Development Centre Studies

# FDI from Developing Countries

## A VECTOR FOR TRADE AND DEVELOPMENT

*by*

Byung-Hwa Lee

OECD

DEVELOPMENT CENTRE OF THE ORGANISATION
FOR ECONOMIC CO-OPERATION AND DEVELOPMENT

# ORGANISATION FOR ECONOMIC CO-OPERATION AND DEVELOPMENT

Pursuant to Article 1 of the Convention signed in Paris on 14th December 1960, and which came into force on 30th September 1961, the Organisation for Economic Co-operation and Development (OECD) shall promote policies designed:

- to achieve the highest sustainable economic growth and employment and a rising standard of living in Member countries, while maintaining financial stability, and thus to contribute to the development of the world economy;
- to contribute to sound economic expansion in Member as well as non-member countries in the process of economic development; and
- to contribute to the expansion of world trade on a multilateral, non-discriminatory basis in accordance with international obligations.

The original Member countries of the OECD are Austria, Belgium, Canada, Denmark, France, Germany, Greece, Iceland, Ireland, Italy, Luxembourg, the Netherlands, Norway, Portugal, Spain, Sweden, Switzerland, Turkey, the United Kingdom and the United States. The following countries became Members subsequently through accession at the dates indicated hereafter: Japan (28th April 1964), Finland (28th January 1969), Australia (7th June 1971), New Zealand (29th May 1973), Mexico (18th May 1994), the Czech Republic (21st December 1995), Hungary (7th May 1996), Poland (22nd November 1996), Korea (12th December 1996) and the Slovak Republic (14th December 2000). The Commission of the European Communities takes part in the work of the OECD (Article 13 of the OECD Convention).

*The Development Centre of the Organisation for Economic Co-operation and Development was established by decision of the OECD Council on 23rd October 1962 and comprises twenty-two Member countries of the OECD: Austria, Belgium, Canada, the Czech Republic, Denmark, Finland, France, Germany, Greece, Iceland, Ireland, Italy, Korea, Luxembourg, Mexico, the Netherlands, Norway, Portugal, Slovak Republic, Spain, Sweden, Switzerland, as well as Argentina and Brazil from March 1994, Chile since November 1998 and India since February 2001. The Commission of the European Communities also takes part in the Centre's Advisory Board.*

*The purpose of the Centre is to bring together the knowledge and experience available in Member countries of both economic development and the formulation and execution of general economic policies; to adapt such knowledge and experience to the actual needs of countries or regions in the process of development and to put the results at the disposal of the countries by appropriate means.*

\*

\* \*

*Publié en français sous le titre :*
**L'IDE des pays en développement**
UN VECTEUR D'ÉCHANGES ET DE CROISSANCE

# Foreword

This publication falls into the Development Centre's work on the Integration of Developing Countries into the World Trading System, and draws on earlier research into the role of foreign direct investment on development. Since the project began, the major country studied, Korea, has become a Member country of the OECD.

# Table of Contents

# Preface

In his *New Forms of International Investment in Developing Countries* (OECD Development Centre, 1984) Charles Oman scrutinised FDI flows primarily from OECD Member countries to developing ones and to emerging economies and differentiated them into direct ownership, joint ventures, licensing, management and production–sharing contracts, international subcontracting, and turnkey operations. He also showed how each type of FDI had different effects on the sovereignty, management and international liabilities of firms.

Byung Hwa Lee, formerly of the Development Centre and now of the Ministry of Planning and Budget in the Republic of Korea, considered the impact of outward FDI flows from developing countries on their own economies. Korea, which has become an OECD Member since Lee's research began, was an early leader among the emerging economies in outward FDI. There is, therefore an accumulation of data and experience that makes the country particularly suitable for study.

Lee's interest on the subject began when he was working at the Centre in the mid–1990s and later developed into a doctoral thesis awarded by the Institut d'Études Politiques, Paris, in 2000. Originally, the research concentrated solely on Korea and was heavily oriented towards an historical analysis. By the beginning of 2000, however, the scale and scope of Korean FDI had become clear, as had the activities of other emerging economies in this sphere. Moreover, Lee's data set could benefit from hindsight and from a high level of verifiability. Accordingly, we asked him to extend his research beyond the strictly Korean context to take in the experience of other countries and to make some theoretical extensions leading to policy recommendations.

What he finds is that firms from emerging economies integrate FDI into their business strategies, particularly in their search for markets. This, in part, explains why Korean firms invested not only in emerging markets and neighbouring developing countries, but also in OECD countries, despite the high levels of competition from local and OECD–area firms. In addition, a significant incentive has been to acquire technology, research and development facilities and trained staff. Where delocalisation may have been important in some developing countries, more often FDI was used for integrating production, management and distribution strategies across all the partners. The result was increased robustness.

A particular contribution that this work makes to our understanding of the dynamics, mechanisms and influence of FDI in (and from) developing countries is the initiation of an enhanced methodology for studying the phenomenon. Lee goes further than the traditional approach in suggesting analysis of the impact on the home economy as a much more significant variable than it is in older industrialised economies. He also proposes much closer examination of the individual determinants of FDI strategies in developing economies.

This book shows that, in spite of their insignificant impact in global markets, FDI outflows from developing countries or emerging economies have a strong domestic impact. This has been observed in several European countries prior to their entry into the Union, but has not been looked at in other contexts.


Jorge Braga de Macedo
President
OECD Development Centre

Avril 2002

# Chapter 1

# Introduction

This book analyses multinational firms with a focus on foreign direct investment (FDI) by firms based in developing and newly emerging economies. Its empirical findings are based on a detailed study of foreign investment activity by the Korean electronics industry, using a rich database developed for that industry during the 1990s. Analysis of the data sheds considerable light on how firms in the industry have invested abroad, their motivations for doing so and the effects of their foreign subsidiaries' operations on home–country exports. This experience offers both lessons and policy guidelines for firms and governments in developing economies as they globalise via FDI.

Multinational business is, of course, a global phenomenon. Year after year, industries have increasingly extended their international operations. This has brought increased economic interdependence among countries and intensified global competition, in response to which firms have developed strategies to serve globally integrated markets. Firms carry out their strategies through various modes: international trade, foreign direct investment (FDI) and strategic alliances. Among these modes, FDI has increased most noticeably. In the past, firms invested abroad mainly to improve exports through commercial presence or to exploit technological advantages by establishing production subsidiaries for local sales. Today, however, they invest abroad increasingly to enter new markets, exploit or enhance their technological and organisational advantages and reduce global business costs and risks.

Trade, the most traditional mode, has also evolved rapidly and in several directions. The composition of world trade by product category has changed substantially. The share of trade in products intensive in capital and technology, such as machinery and transport equipment, has risen continuously. As global production systems have dispersed, international sourcing of intermediate inputs and intra–firm trade has also accounted for increasing shares of total trade.

Strategic alliances, a new business strategy, aim at enhancing competitive advantages *vis–à–vis* competitors through a mutual sharing of technology, managerial assets and resources. The most frequently cited factors behind the recent upsurge in alliances are technological — the increasing costs of R&D in technologically advanced industries and the increasing importance of knowledge in new technologies. The need to share marketing strengths also is occasionally cited. Strategic alliances once were associated with various forms of FDI, including non–equity agreements, minority equity participation and jointly owned subsidiaries. Yet, unlike the formation of joint ventures or establishing foreign subsidiaries, an FDI element is not managerially necessary in strategic alliances (OECD, 1993a).

In line with these changing patterns of international operations, FDI has continued to gain importance as firms come to rely more on it. FDI flows grew more rapidly than international trade during most of the past three decades, especially during the latter half of the 1980s. No available equivalent indicator measures the upsurge of strategic alliances on a flow basis, but a look at figures on royalties and fees as a proxy suggests that FDI growth has remained far in the lead[1].

Firms perform assembly functions at locations where they can most efficiently source inputs from suppliers and deliver final products to target markets. They also can carry out various functions, e.g. production, research and development, marketing, finance and accounting, in geographically separate countries, but this requires establishing foreign affiliates through FDI, which serves as the underlying instrument for the globalisation of corporate activities. The premise for such globalisation is the division of firms' functions into several segments. To describe this, Porter (1986) developed the concept of the value chain, which represents a series of different steps and functions in productive activity that can be ordered in terms of stages of value added.

Because the value chain is discrete, firms can divide it into segments and carry out some of them in different countries. The tremendous progress of information and telecommunications technology has enabled firms to manage, control and co–ordinate subsidiaries deployed in this way (OECD, 1993b). Firms thus can perform some functions in the most favourable locations or pursue the rationalisation of international production. They can avoid duplication of functions among subsidiaries, to reduce unit and total production costs as much as possible.

Firms can specialise in segments of the value chain in which they have strong competitive advantages and depend on other firms to handle the other segments, through international outsourcing and strategic alliances. As global competition has intensified, firms have adopted this strategy more widely. On the other hand, firms also have a tendency to internalise core functions as much as possible. They may internalise upstream activities to seek stable parts supplies, avoid switching costs, saving on joint costs, etc. (Porter, 1986). They may try to internalise downstream activities to keep marketing, distribution and after–sales services under their control, making them less dependent on other firms and giving them more bargaining power in negotiations.

Seen in this light, two factors have driven the globalisation of corporate activities. First, firms shift more segments of value chains out of their home countries and into the target markets, either to reduce labour costs or to enhance market proximity. Second, they establish their foreign subsidiaries to keep some segments of the value chain within the firm, to exploit or enhance core competencies. Depending on its activities in the target market, a firm's globalisation involves horizontal and/or vertical integration. Horizontal integration implies that firms perform nearly the same functions in different locations. Vertical integration involves the spatial dispersion of functions located at different points along the value chain of a particular product.

A particular global configuration of functional activities finds justification in the expected contribution to the overall performance of the corporate system (Doz, 1987). Because a large number of business units can share some core functions, firms can invest abroad to extend segments of the value chain, although this would not be viable or desirable for the performance of an individual business unit. In fact, the new global FDI strategy exploits the advantages of various economies including scale and scope economies (Hax and Majluf, 1991).

Scale economies arise in both plants and firms. At the plant level they relate to such tangible investments as buildings and machinery and equipment, while at the firm level they relate to intangible investment in R&D, management, marketing expertise and the like. Economies of scope can be internal and external. Internally, they occur when a plant can exploit potential cost benefits from the joint production of a diverse range of products. Firms can benefit through sharing technological know-how and working skills between one process or product and another. External economies may derive from externalities of know-how, which appear from increased knowledge and improved information accompanying the expansion of a firm. Economies of both scope and scale have a complementary relationship.

The major modes of international operation are substitutable in serving foreign markets. They link closely, however, and FDI increasingly accompanies the others. International sourcing, for instance, used to be carried out through trade and investment. Global R&D activities often associate with the acquisition of foreign firms and investment in technological alliances. Particularly in recent decades, the changed pattern of trade has often been associated with investment. Intra-firm trade (IFT) and international sourcing of intermediate inputs account for a large part of total trade. They associate mostly with increasing global production through investment. A clear understanding of the FDI-trade relationship is necessary to explain this new trade pattern.

Vertically and horizontally integrated production both involve flows of intermediate goods and materials across borders. Their success depends critically on the ability of firms to trade components and other inputs to final assembly locations, and to export the finished products to world markets (United Nations, 1993). Vertical FDI generates complementary flows of finished goods from foreign affiliates to parent companies and of headquarters services from parents to affiliates. If production is divided into upstream and downstream activities, the FDI-trade relationship can develop further, with parent-to-affiliate exports of intermediate inputs. In the same manner, horizontal FDI also has complementary effects on trade when firms invest in downstream affiliates (Brainard, 1993).

Some limited data show that IFT relates closely with global production systems (Bonturi and Fukasaku, 1993). Globalisation has led firms to use it to move important components and parts to final assembly and to send finished products to final markets. Intra–industry trade (IIT), the exchange between firms of goods and services within the same product category, has also increased, owing partly to increasing investment within the same sector and partly to increased worldwide competition and product differentiation. It also reflects the growing similarity of national production structures as industries globalise their operations.

Related statistics show the importance of FDI in international trade. Total sales of foreign affiliates exceed exports of goods and non–factor services. A substantial portion of world trade takes place within transnational corporate networks. To compare the importance of transactions associated with international production with that of arm's length exports, intra–firm exports should be subtracted from world exports and added to transactions associated with FDI. In such comparisons, only about one–third of international transactions is not associated with FDI (Lee, 2000).

The globalisation of corporate activities does not occur exclusively among firms from developed countries. Some firms in developing countries have increasingly extended their engagement in FDI for the same purposes. Asian new industrialising economies (NIEs) have become major investors in some Southeast Asian developing countries such as China, Viet Nam and Cambodia. Korean firms, unlike other developing country firms, have made aggressive investments in the manufacturing sectors of both developing and developed countries. For some leading Korean conglomerates, Europe is the main target of green–field investments, while the United States is the major target for M&A investment.

This emerging pattern of FDI raises various questions. What has motivated those firms to invest abroad, not only in developing countries but also in developed ones? The motivations stem apparently not only from low costs in the developing countries, but also from the desire for market access and technology in the developed countries. In the latter case, how do they survive under intensified competition in the developed markets? Massive investment abroad will eventually shift production capacity from home to foreign countries. If so, what impact will those investments have on the domestic economy, especially on exports from the home country?

Despite its enormous effect on domestic economies and its strong policy implications, past studies have ignored FDI as a vehicle for the globalisation of corporate activities of firms in less–developed countries (developing countries). Numerous studies have looked at related issues, particularly the determinants and effects of FDI, but most neglect that FDI can perform different functions. To discover its distinctive features requires a new approach that recognises FDI as a vehicle for distributing different functions in different countries.

This study attempts to develop such an approach. It looks at the dynamics of FDI in the course of illustrating how developing country firms distribute their value chains abroad and how technological changes and host–country trade policies affect the spatial distribution of their value chains. It then categorises FDI, by the purpose of investment, into four types: vertical integration, voluntary horizontal integration, non–voluntary horizontal integration and delocalisation. Using this analytical framework, and notwithstanding data limitations, the study then attempts to:

— Identify factors determining the choice of entry modes by examining the functional relationship between modes of subsidiaries and three sets of exogenous variables, namely factors specific to firms, markets and products;

— Investigate the differences in determinants across different types of FDI and identify the critical determinants for each type of FDI;

— Analyse the dynamic effects of foreign production on exports from the home country by separating various facets of the causal relationship between foreign production and export from the home country; and

— Examine the differences in effect across various types of FDI, to draw policy implications relevant for international organisations as well as individual governments.

To recapitulate: these microeconomic activities are a major force shaping the globalisation of industry, and they result in strong linkages between FDI and trade. They basically involve distributing corporate activities in the most favourable locations and/or rationalising production in a global context. Firms can exploit advantages accrued from the optimal spatial deployment of their functions. They also can enjoy various economies, including those of scale and scope, at not only the plant but also the firm level. Firms engage in horizontal integration because of market factors and scale economies, especially at the firm level. In contrast, they pursue vertical integration because of differences in factor cost and scale economies at both the plant and the firm level.

The globalisation of corporate activities also means the global distribution of various functions, not only production but also research and development, marketing, finance and accounting. Firms establish foreign affiliates through FDI in order to distribute their functions geographically. FDI thus is an underlying instrument for the globalisation of corporate activities. Because the value chain representing a series of different steps and functions of a firm's business operations is discrete and internationally divisible, its fragmented segments can be performed in different countries. This enables firms to maintain global production through the combination of horizontal and vertical integration and to establish global production networks primarily on a regional or sub–regional basis.

# Note

1.    UNCTAD, *World Investment Report*, various issues.

# PART ONE

# THE FDI DYNAMIC IN THE GLOBALISATION OF DEVELOPING COUNTRY FIRMS

The rapid development of telecommunication and transportation technologies enables firms to distribute their value chains globally to improve their international competitiveness. Intensified global competition leads them to rely more on FDI as a key vehicle for this distribution of their functions in different countries. Yet FDI by even one firm is not homogenous across regions. An R&D investment in one country, for example, differs greatly from FDI for manufacturing in another, in its determinants as well as its effects. FDI cannot be explained without identifying which segment of its value chain a firm shifts, yet few studies of FDI have noted how FDI can vary for different segments of the value chain.

Part One of the study begins with Chapter 2, with a focus on explaining fundamental differences across main segments of the value chain, differences that might determine the spatial distribution of firms' activities. Based on this discussion, it suggests a logical primary deployment of foreign subsidiaries performing different functions. External and internal factors, however, render the primary deployment of the value chain changeable. Restrictive trade policies of major trading partners as well as investment incentives may have a significant spatial impact. Technology development, especially the application of a new production system, can change the factor intensity of production and thus affect the location of production facilities. Chapters 3 and 4 discuss dynamic aspects of how these two factors affect changes in the location of the value chain. Chapter 5 incorporates these arguments and suggests a diagram to explain some of the dynamic features of FDI in the globalisation of developing country firms.

# Chapter 2

# Major Segments of the Value Chain and Their Spatial Deployment[1]

## Different Attributes

Although firms' value chains can be broken up in many different ways, one can identify several main segments: R&D, core processing or key parts manufacturing, sub–assembly and components manufacturing, final assembly, marketing and sales, and physical distribution and after–sales services[2]. These segments differ in factor intensity, with strong implications for where firms should locate their functions internationally. The most common premise of profit maximisation is that firms will locate their functions optimally in terms of the relevant factor costs in host countries.

R&D, core processing and key parts manufacturing, and international marketing are in general more intensive in technology and knowledge, while assembly and components manufacturing are less so. R&D activities require highly educated workers and thus are intensive in human capital. Basic manufacturing is more diverse, but it certainly is less intensive in human capital than R&D. The accumulation of experience in production is most significant in the assembly function, which makes labour more important than other factors for this function. For these reasons, firms place R&D activities in developed countries with qualified workforces and locate assembly activities in developing countries to reduce labour costs.

In addition to variations in factor intensity, functions are subject to differences in economic scale. Some activities can be compatible with global operations, while others are suitable on a national scale. The key challenge in globalisation is to determine which functions to centralise and which to decentralise. Bartlett (1984) characterised the consumer electronics industry as one in which upstream activities such as R&D and parts manufacturing are suitable to a global scale whereas downstream activities such as marketing and after–sales services are appropriate to a national scale. Assembly activity seems to have intermediate scale economies.

Figure 2.1 shows the differences in economic scale among main segments of the value chain. Heavy R&D expenditures for developing new products and the significant economic scale of parts manufacturing tend to push firms towards global operations (Jun, 1985). By shifting these functions from headquarters to foreign subsidiaries, firms can achieve flexibility in meeting local demand — but losing the advantages of economic scale increases the cost of these functions. Poorly co–ordinated R&D operations might be especially wasteful and thus weaken the global competitive position of firms in developing new technology.

Figure 2.1. **Size of Scale Economies across the Value Chain in the Electronics Industry**

| Value-added Chain | National | Intermediate | Global |
|---|---|---|---|
| R&D | | | ▓ |
| Core Processing & Key Parts Manufacturing | | ▓ | ▓ |
| Sub-assembly & Components Manufacturing | | ▓ | |
| Final Assembly | | ▓ | |
| Marketing | ▓ | ▓ | |
| Physical Distribution | ▓ | | |
| After-sales Services | ▓ | | |

Note:    Shaded areas represent the corresponding economic scale for each segment of the value chain.
Source:   Adopted from the concept in Jun (1985) and modified by the author.

Assembly activity once was sensitive to economic scale. In most cases, however, the efficient capacity for final assembly tends to be smaller than the optimal plant size for component production (Bartlett and Ghosgal, 1989). The introduction of new production technology has changed the optimal capacity of assembly facilities, increasing the flexibility of smaller–scale operations. Marketing, physical distribution and after–sales services clearly need to be responsive to heterogeneous local conditions. Some marketing activities, such as improving brand reputation worldwide, can be global in scale, but most of these functions serve to meet local demand and tastes. Their scale economies are national. Table 2.1 summarises the differences in factor intensity and economic scale across the main segments of the value chain.

In addition to factor intensity and economic scale, the need for market proximity also varies across main segments of the value chain. Some products need more consumer service than others do. Accordingly, firms tend to distribute activities requiring high consumer service closer to the market, which clearly affects the geographical configuration of the value chain. Upstream functions generally have fewer consumer service requirements than downstream ones. As Porter (1986) pointed out, upstream and supporting activities, such as technology development, procurement and logistics, can be debundled from markets, while downstream activities like marketing, physical distribution and after–sales services need to be close to them.

Table 2.1. **Differences in Factor Intensity and Economies of Scale across Main Segments of the Value Chain**

| Factor Intensity (K/L & T) | Economic Scale | | |
| --- | --- | --- | --- |
| | National | Intermediate | Global |
| Capital & Technology Intensive | Marketing | Sub Assembly | R&D<br>Core Processing & Key Parts Manufacturing |
| Intermediate | After-sales Services | Final Assembly | Components Manufacturing |
| Labour Intensive | Physical Distribution | Bulky Components Manufacturing | |

Marketing should be responsive to local tastes in order to satisfy more sophisticated consumers. It functions better when it locates in the market. As after–sales services become increasingly important, especially for sophisticated products, firms can better position themselves in marketing with this function operating inside the target market. Consumers may view this as a commitment to ensuring quick response to their demands. Physical distribution and after–sales services should by nature be contiguous to local markets to perform efficiently.

Upstream activities are geared towards the firm itself or to other producers, while downstream activities target the general public. Upstream functions have fewer customers than downstream functions, and the customers that they do serve spend more time and money on the analysis of products than do general–public consumers. More keen on price and quality, they behave more rationally; hence market proximity to customers is less essential for upstream activities than for those downstream (Figure 2.2).

Figure 2.2. **The Need for Market Proximity across Main Segments of the Value Chain**

| Value-added Chain | High | Intermediate | Low |
| --- | --- | --- | --- |
| R&D | | | ▓ |
| Core Processing & Key Parts Manufacturing | | ▓ | |
| Sub-assembly & Components Manufacturing | | ▓ | |
| Final Assembly | | ▓ | |
| Marketing | ▓ | | |
| Physical Distribution | ▓ | | |
| After-sales Services | ▓ | | |

*Note:*    Shaded areas represent the corresponding degrees of market proximity for each segment of the value chain.

Other factors also can lead to a spatial specialisation of upstream activities. Firms can centralise R&D activities not only to exploit economies of scale but also to protect against technology leakage to outsiders. Several surveys found that most R&D performed by multinational corporations (MNCs) remained concentrated in their home countries. In 1980, for example, US manufacturers kept about 90 per cent of their R&D expenditures within the United States. Only a few Japanese firms performed R&D activities outside Japan (Dicken, 1992). Although R&D activities are becoming increasingly globalised, Dicken (1992) sees higher–level research functions still tending to locate near corporate headquarters[3]. Yet there is some contradictory evidence. Some developing country firms have established R&D facilities outside their home countries in recent years, as exemplified by Korean electronics firms (Lee, 2000). Most of their investments in R&D are for the acquisition of foreign technology, however, or to adapt technology or design to local demand.

Component manufacturing does not necessarily locate close to markets because it enjoys lower transportation costs and tariffs. Components are less bulky than final products, making transportation cost less important for the locational decision. In many countries, tariff levels increase with the level of processing ("tariff escalation"); tariff rates tend to be lowest on basic raw materials and highest on finished goods. Some leading firms also try to put the supply of key components under the control of their parent companies to avoid the risk of being locked in inflexibility, preferring international sourcing for other components. Firms thus probably tend to invest abroad more for assembly than for components manufacturing.

**Logical Deployment of the Value Chain**

Because of differences not only in economic scale and scope but also in their need for geographical proximity to markets, research and product–development functions generally demand high global integration, while distribution and after–sales services require high national responsiveness. Other functions should also reconcile their varying needs for national differentiation, better marketing and global integration, to exploit economies of scale. The final–assembly function should be more responsive to national differentiation than to global integration. Sub–assembly and component manufacturing has similar characteristics, but compared with final assembly it should focus somewhat more on global integration while not neglecting the need for national differentiation. For core processing and key parts manufacturing, on the other hand, market differentiation may be generally less important than global integration. The design function falls within R&D, but design modification to reflect local tastes or technical specification might require some national responsiveness.

Based on the foregoing discussion, one can construct a diagram to show graphically the varying needs for global integration and national differentiation across activities. Figure 2.3 demonstrates simply how downstream activities should be more responsive to market differences than upstream activities. The latter require more integrated operations to exploit their economic potential, including scale economies.

Figure 2.3. **Conceptual Contour for the Spatial Distribution of the Value-chain**

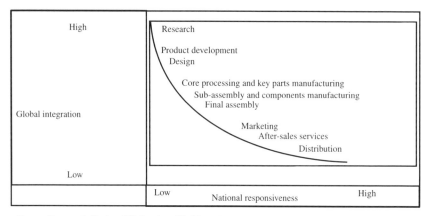

*Source:* Concepts in Bartlett (1984) and modified by author.

Firms deploy subsidiaries for downstream activities such as marketing in numerous target markets but locate upstream functions, with broader geographical responsibilities, in the domestic market or only a few foreign countries. By deploying the value chain in this way, they can obtain competitive advantages in cost reduction derived from partial or complete global integration of upstream activities and from a wider distribution of downstream activities. Yet Figure 2.3 does not necessarily imply that all industries follow the same pattern. They may have differences in factor intensity for the same function. Some are less sensitive to labour costs than others in certain activities. The cost of linking physically separated value chains varies with production technology, and not all industries can reduce linkage costs to the same extent. Some should integrate production in one place because physical separation of the value chain would seriously undermine their competitiveness, but others can easily separate and link these operations without much additional cost. In general, the more stabilised technologies have lower linkage costs.

The major finding of an OECD sector survey and study of globalisation was that the general pattern of industrial globalisation varies among generic groups of industries, i.e. science–based groups, scale–intensive groups and groups intensive in resources and labour (OECD, 1993*b*). The pattern of physical separation of firms' value chains differs similarly across industries. Several product–specific factors also affect value chain distribution. Trade barriers and transportation costs vary from product to product. Final products tend to be more often subject to trade barriers and more sensitive to transport cost than parts and components. Among components, bulky parts need to locate closer to assemblers while small, common components do not. Some products may require more consumer services like advertising or after–sales service than others, and some products need more differentiation across markets. Firms must have "close to market" operating modes for products requiring high consumer service and differentiation. In general, consumer products should be more sensitive to local tastes and demand and thus require more consumer service and differentiation than industrial products.

Given that both industry–specific and product–specific factors affect the spatial deployment of foreign subsidiaries, Figure 2.4 integrates the effects conceptually. It extends the logic of Figure 2.3. On the left it shows differences across electronics products in economic scale and need for market proximity. Colour television receivers (CTVs) and videocassette recorders (VCRs) need higher market responsiveness than their components, such as printed circuit boards (PCBs) and colour picture tubes (CPTs). CPTs need more global integration than TVs and VCRs because of differences in economic scale. The right–hand side of the diagram reveals differences in economic scale and the need for market proximity across functions for some consumer electronic products like CTVs and VCRs. These industries are highly scale–intensive, with rapidly decreasing unit production costs. R&D expenditures remain very important for leading–edge firms. Sales generally are very price–sensitive, with fierce competition for market share by minimising costs. Trade barriers significantly affect market access.

Figure 2.4. **Conceptual Contour for the Deployment of the Value-chain**

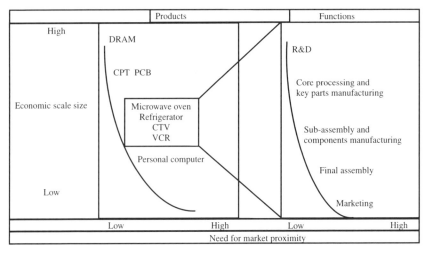

*Source:* Same as Figure 2.3.

This understanding of the value chain and its distribution helps to explain the massive investments in the electronics industry during the last two decades from developed to developing countries — the delocalisation of assembly facilities for low–end electronic products and of common electronic parts production facilities[4]. The main motive for delocalisation is to enhance competitiveness through lower production costs. Given the relatively high proportion of wage costs in certain segments of the value chain, firms have an incentive to locate production in developing countries with low–cost but adequately trained workforces (OECD, 1994).

## Sequential Deployment of the Value Chain

A sequential process in the deployment of the value chain can explain the dynamic aspect of FDI more distinctively. Many studies reveal that firms tend to adopt gradual and evolutionary approaches in foreign markets, because incremental involvement lowers the perceived risks owing mainly to their lack of knowledge and resources (Johanson and Vahlne, 1977). Firms can extend their international involvement step by step as they accumulate more market–specific knowledge and experience.

Several studies of Swedish multinational corporations (MNCs) in the 1970s found a sequence in international operations. Starting from an initial position of no regular exports to a foreign market, firms approached the market first through an independent representative (agent), then with a sales subsidiary and ultimately with local foreign production. Several surveys have found that no firm has started production in a foreign country without having sold its products in the country beforehand. According to Johanson and Vahlne (1977), a firm's internationalisation takes two directions: increasing involvement in an individual foreign country and the successive establishment of foreign operations in several countries. Development occurs in one of these directions only in extreme cases. The most common pattern is to expand international operations in both directions concurrently.

As the firm increases its involvement in a country, the flow of value–added activities shifts increasingly out of the home country into the target market — but not necessarily so. Firms can establish subsidiaries in target markets either to expand functions performed in the home market or to start new value–added activities that they do not conduct in their home markets. This serves to focus their internalisation of value–added activities to a greater extent in the target markets.

Although the evolutionary pattern described above is considered as most typical of the internationalisation process, the establishment of foreign subsidiaries seems to have a sequence as well. The Uppsala researchers developed the concept of psychic distance to explain it (Nördstrom, 1991). Psychic distance, different from physical distance, represents how firms perceive opportunities, given obstacles to the free flow of information to and from a country. Firms seem to have a strong propensity to establish foreign subsidiaries initially in countries with low psychic distance from their home countries and to expand additional establishments gradually to more distant markets. Several other studies have found some variation in the pattern of international operations among firms as well as industries. Even within the same firm the pattern can change over time. One survey found that the time difference between the establishment of consecutive foreign subsidiaries decreased over time (Hedlund and Kverneland, 1984). The evolutionary process that characterises firms' international operations implies an order or sequence in deploying the value chain. The most common path that firms follow begins with the establishment of marketing subsidiaries for local sales. Subsequent stages include assembly, parts manufacturing and then regionally integrated production with regional headquarters establishments and R&D subsidiaries in major markets.

Figure 2.5 illustrates the most probable path of changing international operations and a more detailed elaboration of the evolutionary process. Its vertical axis indicates levels of internalisation within a firm's subsidiaries, while the horizontal axis represents the value chain level shifted to the target market. Levels of internalisation rise with the value chain shifts. In this formulation, the first stage of international operation shifts downstream activities to foreign countries. Prior to this stage, firms must accumulate related production technology. With the accumulation of experience and technology in the domestic market, they can start their international operations. At first, they export through domestic or foreign trading agents, and outsiders conduct all downstream functions. Firms have no power to control marketing in the target markets. As exports increase, firms tend to shift from exporting through agents to local sales (still exports) by marketing subsidiaries. The major motive for this shift is to bring marketing, distribution and after–sales services under their control.

Figure 2.5. **Sequential Process of International Operations**

| Level of internalisation within subsidiaries in the target markets | | | |
|---|---|---|---|
| High | | | Regional integrating ↑ R & D ↗ |
| Intermediate | | Core processing and key parts manufacturing ↗ Sub-assembly and components manufacturing ↑ Local final assembly | |
| Low | Local sales ↗ ↑ Exports from home countries | | |
| | Downstream | Midstream | Upstream |

Level of value-chain shifted to the target market

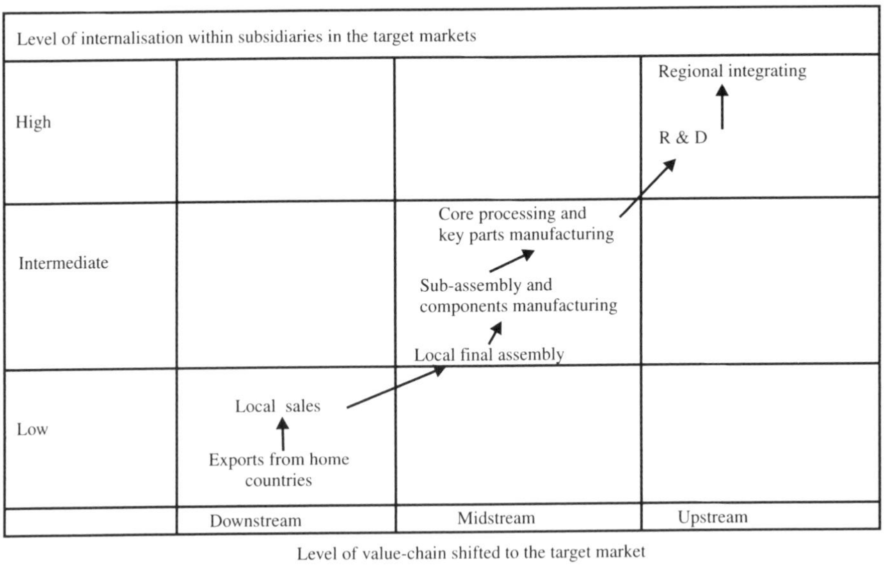

*Source:* Concepts in Jun (1985) and modified by author.

The second stage involves foreign production. As firms accumulate experience in target markets through marketing subsidiaries, they tend to shift not only marketing but also some production to their major target markets. Final assembly may move first, followed by some common components manufacturing. In contrast, core parts design, development and manufacturing all would be retained in the home country. As more local and foreign firms enter a target market, competition intensifies. In response, firms tend to commit further, putting most of their production activities in the target markets to maintain low–cost advantages. Local manufacturing of core components and similar new local functions thus begin.

The third stage highlights differential local market strategies and the integration of foreign operations. With more market–specific knowledge, firms can shift R&D functions to local markets to meet specific local demands. Indeed, at this stage the internalisation of all remaining functions occurs within the subsidiaries, and firms normally are establishing foreign operations successively in various markets in order to optimise resource distribution globally in response to intensified global competition. Yet this broad distribution of core corporate functions to many distant affiliates raises problems of co–ordination and integration. In response, firms now establish regional headquarters to integrate international operations, including management, financial control, production and process R&D, production and marketing. Synergies can arise in such integration through sharing common functions of subsidiaries as well as experience and knowledge that they have accumulated.

The sequential process of distributing the value chain can coincide with the appropriate location for it over the product life cycle (Jun, 1985). At the innovative stage of a product when its market and technology are unstable, firms need to communicate frequently, internally and within the market. They perform better when most of their activities remain located close to the home market. Over time, as the technology stabilises, firms have less need to communicate but now become sensitive to factor costs. This is when assembly functions may shift to target markets to take advantages of lower factor costs and market proximity. R&D and parts–manufacturing functions likely remain in the home market.

When the product becomes fully standardised and the technology completely stabilised, production cost becomes most critical, especially with strong competition. Parts manufacturing may now join assembly activities abroad. The most appropriate locations will be the countries with the lowest costs. Table 2.2 shows the general relationship between logical host–country candidates for various functions and the stages of the product life cycle. It shows how location decisions can change over time. The most favourable locations shift from the home country to the target market or to least–cost countries as the product life cycle moves towards maturity. Major target markets are countries or regions whose markets and/or market potentials are large. The least–cost country varies in accordance with factor intensity and the level of required technology for each value–added activity. As products reach maturity and become standard, their production technology will diffuse, making developing countries the most likely favourable locations for midstream activities.

Developing country firms also will likely follow the product life cycle in localising certain products. Assembly is the first production activity that they internalise in the domestic market. Later, they produce common parts earlier than core parts because it is much easier. They localise core–parts production gradually with the accumulation of experience and technology. This process of localisation in the domestic market extends to their expansion abroad. developing country firms establish marketing and assembly subsidiaries much earlier than upstream subsidiaries. Because they internalise core–parts manufacturing late at home due to difficulties in acquiring technology, and because they are averse to the high risk of heavy investment often associated with foreign production of core parts, they tend to retain this function at headquarters as long as possible (Kang and Chang, 1987). They establish core–parts manufacturing subsidiaries much later than other types of subsidiaries.

Table 2.2. **Appropriate Locations for Value-chain Functions over the Product Life Cycle**

| Value-chain | Stage of Product Life Cycle | | |
| --- | --- | --- | --- |
| | Innovative | Mature | Standardised |
| Regional Headquarters | Home Country | Home Country | Major Markets |
| R&D | Home Country | Home Country | Home Country |
| Core Processing & Key Parts | Home Country | Home Country | Home/ Least Cost |
| Sub-assembly & Components | Home Country | Home Country | Least Cost Country |
| Final Assembly | Home Country | Target Market | Target Market |
| Marketing | Home/Target | Target Market | Target Market |

*Source:*    Concepts in Jun (1985) as modified by the author.


The sequential process of expanding international operations implies that downstream subsidiaries will be established early, but all of them will not necessarily develop into upstream subsidiaries. As noted earlier, firms tend to centralise upstream activities and decentralise downstream activities because of differences in the need for national responsiveness and for global integration among them. As a result, firms will likely establish more downstream than upstream subsidiaries.


# Notes


1.    Some of the arguments in this chapter on different characteristics across the value chain and on the development process of foreign subsidiaries are drawn from Jun (1985).

2.    These segments are very similar to the stages of the value chain proposed by Ernst (1997).

3.    Dicken (1992) divides R&D activities into support laboratories, locally integrated R&D laboratories and interdependent international R&D laboratories. He maintains that the locational needs of R&D facilities depend on the particular type of R&D. Lower–level support laboratories are more closely related to the firm's production units whereas higher–level R&D operations tend to be located independently.

4.    In the strict sense of the term, delocalisation means the transfer of production units coupled with the closure of domestic production units.

# Chapter 3

# The Impact of Restrictive Trade Policy
# on the Spatial Deployment of the Value Chain

## Strong Linkages between FDI and Trade

Although FDI and international trade theories developed separately, some models integrating them have appeared since the early 1980s. They relax the restrictive hypothesis that a firm produces goods and services in one location and acknowledge that firms can own and employ factors located in different countries. They divide the activities of firms into headquarters activities, including R&D, and the actual production process, including upstream production for intermediate goods and downstream production for finished goods. They assume that all activities have increasing returns to scale and the headquarters function can be transferred at no cost, even to distant production facilities. Under these assumptions, firms can separate production facilities geographically from their headquarters. The key issue is how firms deploy production in order to maximise their profits. Production configurations eventually determine FDI and trade patterns as well. The many hypotheses on the subject divide, broadly speaking, into two types of approaches (Brainard, 1993).

The first approach is the factor–proportion hypothesis. It is based on differences in factor endowments across countries and in factor intensity across various segments of the value chain. Some firms can separate their activities geographically to exploit factor–price differentials across countries. Usually, production activities are more labour–intensive while headquarters are more capital–intensive. Therefore, if factor prices are not equalised through trade, firms can relocate their production functions in relatively labour–abundant economies and their headquarters in relatively capital–abundant countries.

The globalisation of a firm's activities depends on how much factor proportions differ across functions and countries and how much the firm can separate its functions geographically. When differences in factor proportions are large enough and factor–cost differentials remain significant owing to the high cost of trade in factors, FDI flows will prevail[1]. When factor endowments are not sufficiently large or trade equalises factor prices, however, firms would have no incentive to invest abroad (Helpman and Krugman, 1985). Furthermore, if FDI were motivated solely by factor–price differentials, it would proceed in a single direction in response to strong factor–proportion differences. This hypothesis can explain FDI for vertical expansion across borders, especially from developed to developing countries (Helpman, 1984; Markusen, 1984).

The second approach is the proximity–concentration hypothesis. It explains the preference for overseas production over exporting as a trade–off between the advantages of proximity to customers and suppliers and those of scale economies (Horstmann and Markusen, 1992). Firms decide by comparing these advantages whether to penetrate foreign markets through trade or through investment.

When factor–proportion differences are not substantial, the configuration of a firm's foreign production depends on the size of scale economies at the plant relative to the firm and the magnitude of transport costs (Brainard, 1993). This hypothesis maintains that FDI will prevail over trade if the ratio of scale economies at the plant relative to the corporate level is low and transport costs and trade barriers are high. It can explain FDI for horizontal expansion across borders to seek better access to markets.

The two approaches are not mutually exclusive. Firms make the decision to produce abroad based on the relative importance of advantages derived from both (Brainard, 1992). Factor–proportion differences increase the likelihood of concentrating production in a single location without proximity advantages. When proximity advantages are sufficiently strong, horizontal multinationals would emerge in the absence of factor–price differences. Because of these differences in motives, some economists argue that horizontal integration dominates when countries have similar relative endowments and when trade costs are significant. Vertical integration, they argue, dominates when countries differ significantly in factor endowments (Markusen, 1996).

Established FDI theory has noted that restrictive trade policy in importing countries would have a positive impact on FDI inflows. As the internalisation theory states, government intervention in the market can create market imperfections, which in turn will create rents for domestic and foreign firms. It attracts rent–seeking investment. Protection acts as the equivalent of an investment subsidy. Host countries can use restrictive trade policy or incentives as alternative ways of attracting rent–seeking FDI. Many empirical studies support these arguments. Lall and Siddharthan (1982), for instance, found that effective protection has determined the industrial composition of foreign direct investment in the United States. Another study found that Korea's limited market opening in insurance in the 1980s attracted rent–seeking investment (Cho, 1988). Similar evidence has been found for outward investment, which will be discussed later.

In contrast, some insist that FDI can also accompany trade liberalisation in the long run. Vertically or horizontally integrated production involves the frequent flow of materials, semi–finished products and components across borders. Therefore, the success of complex integration strategies rests crucially on the ability of firms to trade components and other inputs to locations for final assembly, and to export finished goods to world markets. In recent years, FDI has more frequently associated with such integration strategies. Actually, the growth of FDI takes place increasingly in parallel with the growth of trade. During the 1970s, FDI outflows and exports grew at similar rates; in the second half of the 1980s, the growth of FDI outflows exceeded that of exports.

Based on these trends, some studies conclude that FDI and international trade are complementary means of accessing and supplying domestic markets (UNCTAD, 1992). The contradiction between microeconomic and macroeconomic arguments reflects the complexity of the links between FDI and trade. Some studies conclude that the impact of trade policy on FDI flows is hard to generalise in the long run (OECD, 1991a). Yet if one observes FDI as a strategic corporate response to exploit changing market opportunities or to seek security, a more distinct impact of each trade policy on the spatial distribution of a firm's value chain becomes evident.

## Trade Policies and Their Different Implications for FDI

Trade policies — or trade barriers — can take a variety of forms within the two main categories of tariff and non–tariff barriers (NTBs). The average level of tariffs has declined very substantially, mainly through successive rounds of international negotiation in GATT (now the WTO). In contrast, various forms of NTBs have found increasing use, especially since the mid–1970s. NTBs now may well be more important than tariffs in influencing the levels and composition of trade between countries. Among them, quotas, voluntary export restraints, antidumping, countervailing duties, safeguard actions, technical regulations, local–content rules, government–procurement policies and other market–segmenting policies are frequently cited. This discussion will review some of them to elaborate on the relationship between each and its impact on the spatial distribution of the value chain.

### Standard vs. Contingent Protection

Besides the common distinction between tariffs and NTBs, other ways to classify trade barriers exist. The notions of standard and contingent protection will be useful for this discussion. The former is independent of the performance or behaviour of either domestic or foreign industries. The latter, on the other hand, can be employed only if the behaviour or performance of a domestic industry or foreign industries exporting to the domestic market meets certain pre–specified criteria.

The primitive forms of standard protection are import bans, import licences, and import quotas. They empower governments to control import volume directly. Following multilateral GATT/WTO efforts for trade liberalisation, these forms of trade barriers have been reduced significantly, but some developing countries still resort to standard protection such as high tariffs or quantitative restrictions under GATT Article II–c to protect domestic industries.

Most developed countries have come to rely on wide use of contingent protection, leading some critics to argue that it nullifies the effects of GATT agreements on levels of standard protection (Hindley, 1994). The primary forms of contingent protection under GATT are antidumping actions (Article VI), safeguard actions (Article XIX), and countervailing duties (Article XVI). Recourse to these measures in a manner consistent with related GATT articles calls for fulfilment of certain conditions. A common one is that a domestic industry must be injured non–negligibly[2]. Any country can use such protection in attempts to avoid adverse effects of imports on its domestic industries. Antidumping is the most widely used contingent measure. The conventional economic rationale for it is based on the notions of predatory pricing and discriminating monopoly. Predatory dumping leads to the failure of domestic producers and subsequent exposure of domestic buyers to monopolistic price setting. Hindley (1991) maintains, however, that although there is an economic rationale for antidumping actions, its scope is very small and involves "special cases" which may be resolved by other measures.

Messerlin (1991) also points out that antidumping measures can be applied arbitrarily. Some terms in the antidumping provision are so vague that domestic industries can and do resort to it to avoid import competition. He notes that the "material injury clause", a crucial element in antidumping cases, has never been enforced in an economic manner by the EC. As a result, domestic antidumping legislation tends to distort behaviour, particularly of producers, and contribute to making the world trade environment more uncertain. Faced with the possibility of being subjected to antidumping investigations, exporting firms will tend to reduce exports to the market.

Emergency safeguard actions are authorised by the GATT to counter the adverse effects of surges in imports. They are less frequently used than antidumping actions, chiefly because importing countries must meet various conditions to invoke Article GATT XIX. Some countries maintain that the "serious injury" threshold is too high, the causal link between imports and injury is too difficult to establish and the implicit requirement to pay compensation is too damaging to their trade interests. The major reasons for its non–use, however, lie in the availability of more flexible instruments of protection, such as antidumping and so–called "grey area measures" including voluntary export restraints (VERs) and orderly market arrangements (OMAs).

Two reasons often are cited for the preference of governments of importing countries for VERs over safeguards. First, Article XIX does not allow protection that discriminates between different exporting countries. Second, the GATT allows any exporting country affected by an Article XIX action to claim "compensation". As of May 1993, countries had notified 151 safeguard actions under Article XIX. Almost a third of them had been imposed since the conclusion of the Tokyo Round in 1979. During the ensuing 14 years, the EU made the most frequent use of safeguards, invoking Article XIX a total of 18 times. By contrast, the United States invoked Article XIX safeguards only four times (Scott, 1994).

Countervailing duties (CVDs) are designed to offset the price advantages derived from subsidies in exporting countries. Industry can reduce production cost with a subsidy, which in turn reduces the export price. CVD procedures are basically the same as those for antidumping measures. An importing country can claim injury to a domestic industry from the subsidised exports and impose countervailing duties. With the additional condition that subsidies must exist and the need to show a causal relationship between the subsidies and injury, CVD has been the least frequently used form of contingent protection. The US government has undertaken the greatest number of countervailing duty investigations, while the EU has used them little in comparison with antidumping proceedings.

The different types of contingent protection can substitute for one another because they are all designed to restrict imports. Importing countries can threaten to invoke any one of the GATT provisions among antidumping, safeguard, and countervailing duties to protect domestic industries. Such threats, moreover, may increase their bargaining leverage in negotiations leading to VERs or OMAs. To avoid uncertainty, an exporting country's government and exporting industries often prefer a VER to a legal litigation against a threatened antidumping or a countervailing duty action.

Ozawa (1985) maintained that Japanese diversification in investment from Asian countries to advanced countries was induced mainly by rising contingent protectionism in the United States and Europe. For example, Japan accepted voluntary export restraints on exports of automobiles and semiconductors to the United States in the 1980s to avoid trade action. This VER prompted Japanese investment in major markets, especially the United States, during the second half of the 1980s. Such contingent protection has led to fears about future imposition of trade barriers in other industries and the growing necessity to preserve market access through FDI (UNCTAD, 1995).

### Local–Content Requirements

Local–content requirements (LCRs) stipulate a minimum level of domestic inputs in the manufacturing process through the application of rules of origin that determine the country from which a product originates. Some developing countries require that a certain percentage of specific types of local components be used in foreign–owned manufacturing operations. The most acceptable rationale for this policy is infant–industry protection in developing countries (Greenaway, 1992). Developed countries also use it widely, however, to shield domestic industry from intensified competition. It can take the form of pre–conditions for approval of FDI, but mostly is prescribed as a condition for the extension of preferential treatment, such as subsidies or tax exemptions.

Among various criteria to decide whether the requirements are fulfilled, the most common is the percentage of value added within the country. Products that meet prescribed levels can be treated as domestic; if not they are treated as foreign products. The required percentage differs across products and countries. The NAFTA, for instance, requires 50 per cent local (regional) content to qualify for free–trade treatment. The EU requires 45 per cent of value creation in the region for most products — but 60 per cent for automobiles.

Local–content rules try to ensure or enhance the use of local products and promote fuller integration of foreign investment in the national economy. Yet they can be used as well to restrict domestic market penetration of foreign firms. For instance, a high local–content rule advocated by the United States and several European countries was used mostly to restrict the increasing market share of Japanese cars assembled there. According to Dicken (1992), this stimulated the arrival of more than 300 Japanese component manufacturers in the United States alone.

The economic effect of local–content rules can vary from industry to industry and from country to country and thus is hard to evaluate. Several studies, e.g. Greenaway (1992), have tried. Most conclude that it is difficult to generalise. It nevertheless is obvious that this instrument has some distorting effects on resource allocation. It shifts the cost of higher–priced domestic inputs forward to producers of final goods. To invest even with this disadvantage, there must be offsetting factors, such as threats to market security (Dicken, 1992).

Because of these trade–distorting effects, LCRs were included in the negotiations on trade–related aspects of investment measures (TRIMs) in the Uruguay Round. The LCRs prohibited by the TRIMs agreement include mandatory restrictions enforceable under domestic law or administrative rulings and other prescribed conditions used to secure preferential treatment such as subsidies or tax exemptions. In many countries, LCRs are not mandatory, but foreign affiliates cannot receive tariff exemptions on their products if they fail to meet the level of domestic production that the government requires. That makes LCRs mandatory *de facto* for investing firms.

LCRs also have an impact on the allocation of foreign subsidiaries among countries. Host countries impose LCRs to increase value–added activities of industry within their territory as much as possible. If investing firms perform more value–added activities in the host countries because of these trade policies, they will perform fewer elsewhere. This often conflicts with the firms' global sourcing strategies. In that case, some distortion in resource allocation can arise because of forced local sourcing and production regardless of price and quality.

The relationship between LCRs and the introduction of advanced production technology is controversial. Some may argue that new production technologies, e.g. the lean production system, increase local sourcing because the system requires the proximity of parts suppliers. Therefore, LCRs cannot be a burden on investment using such production systems. In fact, the local sourcing ratio of some successful Korean electronic subsidiaries is much higher than that required. Most of them have already applied new production technologies to a certain degree. This will be discussed more in detail later. On the other hand, Korean experience also reveals that LCRs have adverse affects on the performance of both investments in early stages and investment by companies that do not have such sophisticated production technology. Samsung's and LG's investments for assembly of TV sets in the United States and Haitai's investment for assembly of car stereos in France provide good examples.

## Technical Barriers and Protective IPR policy

Technical regulations include technical standards and certification systems. Many of them serve legitimate purposes, such as ensuring the quality of products, ensuring public health and safety and protecting the environment. Although not intended to restrict trade, they nonetheless may have an adverse impact on it. When standards and certification systems vary significantly across countries, exporters incur additional costs in dealing with them, which unnecessarily restricts imports.

Some standards and certification systems, however, are designed as disguised import restrictions. If a country imposes technical standards that result in substantial additional costs for foreign products, imports may face serious adverse effects. Some countries have implemented standards and certification systems in the name of legitimate objectives, but in fact, use them *de facto* to limit imports or subject them to discriminatory treatment. Such systems are trade–restrictive in themselves.

The harmonisation and transparency of standards and certification systems can mitigate their unnecessarily trade–restrictive effects. The GATT and the International Standards Organisation have worked for years to this end. The GATT has produced a new TBT (technical barriers to trade) agreement that imposes stricter obligations to ensure transparency and conformity with international standards. International efforts are still needed to promote harmonisation, provide more transparency in drafting and administration processes, and ensure equal treatment of domestic and foreign products (WTO, 1994).

Despite the progress that has occurred, these trade issues remain among the major factors affecting the distribution of the value chain. Technical barriers have eased through efforts towards mutual recognition and harmonisation, but new technical standards and regulations constantly appear, especially for emerging electronic products such as HDTV and mobile telecommunication equipment. It is critical for firms developing new products to have advance access to information on anticipated standards and regulations. Without it, they cannot become involved in developing those products.

Like standards and certification systems, intellectual property has trade–related aspects that recently have attracted international attention. Inadequate protection of intellectual property discourages foreign companies from investing or transferring technology. In many developing countries, the insufficient protection of intellectual property rights (IPR) or its inappropriate enforcement remain as major causes of trade friction. Production and distribution of counterfeit goods have long been typical trade issues. In contrast some developed countries maintain newly introduced systems that are too protective. The United States, for instance, introduced a layout–design protection law that protects far more than international law does.

Those countries often maintain protective procedures to enforce their legal IPR regimes — as is the case with arbitrary border enforcement measures not consistent with the GATT or other international agreements. These procedures may also function as non–tariff barriers and thereby restrict trade. As trade in intellectual property is expected to grow further, they will constitute one of the most important trade barriers. To avoid such trade–distorting effects, countries should strive not only to ensure the basic protection of IPR, but also to harmonise their intellectual property regimes.

In response to international demand, the GATT produced the agreement on Trade–Related Aspect of Intellectual Property Rights (TRIPs). Although it establishes valuable minimum standards for IPR protection, some countries still maintain national systems not consistent with the international legal framework. For instance, Section 337 of the US Tariff Act of 1930 aims to exclude from the United States imports in violation of valid US–registered intellectual property rights. The Omnibus Trade and Competitive Act of 1988 removed the requirement of injury in cases involving the infringement of patents, trademarks, copyrights, and layout designs, thus reducing the burden of proving a Section 337 violation. This simplification of procedure made Section 337 an easily accessible remedy for US domestic industries. In 1988, the GATT Council adopted a panel report that concluded that Section 337 procedures violated the national–treatment provision of the GATT agreement. The US government, however, has yet to rectify them.

These kinds of unilateral trade measures seriously undermine the market security of developing country firms. The removal of the injury requirement increases the number of domestic firms filing complaints to prohibit importation into the United States. Even at the filing stage, a trade–dampening effect and uncertainty occur. Furthermore, these issues take a long time to resolve. Developing country firms' exports, especially of technology–intensive products, can easily become uncertain when market security in major importing countries is critical for them. To avoid such insecurity, firms have several ways to respond. Among them, FDI for acquiring or adapting technology is an option. Firms can establish research affiliates or acquire foreign firms to obtain technology. In that sense, trade–related aspects of IPR have a serious impact on FDI as well.

### Regional Economic Integration

Many empirical studies based on customs–union theory have shown that trade diversion follows all the steps in regional economic integration, as in Europe. Similarly, several studies have found that investment diversion may occur (Heitger and Stehn, 1990). Trade and investment diversion relate closely. Regional economic integration attracts investment because the expanded market offers opportunities to exploit economies of scale. More important, the elimination of internal trade barriers provides more opportunities for reorganisation and rationalised investment (Yannopoulos, 1990). At the same time, both increasing trade protection and fears of discrimination against non–member countries lead firms to invest within regional trading blocs to take advantage of the increased protection or to avoid future discrimination (Kreinin, 1992).

Regional economic integration can lead to additional trade barriers, although not necessarily so. It intensifies regional competition, in response to which special interest groups will ask for additional external trade barriers. They may find sympathetic ears in governments of trading–bloc members, which have their own national interests to represent. On balance, regional economic integration tends to result in a reduction of internal non–tariff barriers on the one hand, and in an increase in protection on the other (Heitger and Stehn, 1990).

Major trading blocs often impose high local–content requirements that may affect FDI flows. Measures to discourage investment in "screwdriver plants" (minimal–assembly facilities) require very high levels of value–added in the integrating region for products of such facilities to qualify as domestic. This local–content requirement becomes critical when foreign subsidiaries start to sell their products in other countries in the region, or begin exporting to countries that have special trade agreements with the trading bloc. For example, when a Japanese automotive affiliate in the United Kingdom exported its cars to France, an 80 per cent local–content rule was applied. Such rules induce firms to shift most of the value chain to host countries, thereby increasing investment diversion.

## Trade Policy and the Geographical Deployment of a Firm's Value Chain

Trade policy leads firms to adopt complex strategies. As the discussion above implies, each category of trade policy instruments has a different effect on the distribution of value chains. Effective standard trade protection in some developing countries can be a *de facto* import prohibition of some finished goods. The most common way to bypass these direct trade restrictions is to establish assembly operations in the protected markets. Ozawa (1985) claims that Japanese firms invested in knockdown assembly operations in Asian countries in the early stages to circumvent such trade restrictions. Other studies of FDI, such as those by Culem (1988) and Heitger and Stehn (1990), also suggest that foreign investment may often occur to bypass trade barriers.

Contingent protection, used mostly in major markets such as the EU and the United States, can be employed when exports to a market by a given industry reach a certain level. Developing country firms, whose domestic markets are relatively small, are very vulnerable to the threat of contingent trade measures because they depend heavily on exports to those markets. A way to avoid this market insecurity is to set up local assembly plants, sourcing only bulky parts and components locally and using home–made parts as much as possible. Some studies of Korean FDI found that antidumping, VER, and safeguard measures have indeed triggered FDI in assembly subsidiaries in established markets (Jun, 1987).

There remain some differences between assembly subsidiaries triggered by standard protection and those provoked by contingent protection. The former (offensive) spring up to penetrate new markets, the latter (defensive) to maintain exports to existing markets. Offensive investments often associate with firms' strategies for expansion, i.e. increased sales volume. The key distinction involves whether firms can invest abroad voluntarily. In defensive investment, firms are forced to set up assembly subsidiaries regardless of the availability of proper production systems for the locations concerned. Some firms, on the verge of losing markets, are compelled to invest quickly, without screening possible locational or entry–mode alternatives. Offensive investment, on the other hand, forms a part of firms' growth strategies. Firms have many alternatives and can choose entry modes or find investment locations congenial to their markets and production technologies.

Assembly affiliates often source some bulky parts in host countries to avoid their high transportation costs. Strict local–content rules, however, push firms to shift additional segments of the value chain, mostly common parts production, to host countries. Very high local–content rules induce further shifts, including core–parts production. More broadly, the profitability of assembly subsidiaries set up in response to contingent protection or local–content requirements can be weak, supported only by the use of intermediate inputs imported from home countries. Most such investments have shown poor performance. High local–content requirements often lead these types of foreign ventures to disaster. Most Korean FDI in developed countries in the early stages evidenced these arguments (Han, 1992).

Technical trade barriers and protective IPR policy, on the other hand, lead firms to shift R&D to host countries. The threat of invoking unilateral trade measures has seriously endangered exports from developing country firms and weakened market security, especially for newly developed electronic products. Some developing country firms in those industries are highly vulnerable to these trade policies. The ultimate solution would be the development of their own indigenous technology, but this is not easy to achieve in a short time with their rather weak technological infrastructures. Strategic alliances and cross–technology licences can provide a way to solve trade problems related to IPRs. Most developing country firms, however, do not have special technology to use as leverage for making such agreements and cannot develop it quickly. Thus they have strong incentives to establish research affiliates in developed countries to acquire necessary information or technology as fast as possible. Most leading Korean firms have established new or expanded R&D subsidiaries in the United States or the EU in response to technical barriers or restrictive IPR policies.

Compared with other trade policies, regional economic integration has a more complex impact on the spatial distribution of foreign subsidiaries. Regional economic integration, by nature, provides manifold attractions for FDI. First, the enlarged regional market increases its attraction to market–seeking foreign investment. Second, strict local–content rules, which often follow regional economic integration, attract investment for parts production. Third, the enlarged market allows investing firms to rationalise their operations on a regional basis to take advantage of economies of scale and scope. This leads them to establish regionally integrated networks of affiliates for cross–border affiliate trade. Through such networks, firms can take advantage of differences in production costs among locations and exploit synergy effects in the regional bases more easily (Sauvant *et al.*, 1994).

Figure 3.1 sums up and illustrates the foregoing discussion; its shaded areas represent segments of the value chain most likely to shift successively in response to the imposition of specific host–country trade policies. With no effective host–country protection, firms would shift only the marketing function, to seek the advantages of consumer proximity. Facing standard or contingent protection, firms would first additionally shift the assembly function. Subsequently, if host countries impose local–content requirements and strict technical barriers, investing firms would come under pressure to move parts production and R&D to host countries. Finally, in response to regional integration, firms would shift some corresponding segments of the value chain to take advantage of scale and scope economies or to rationalise their FDI on a regional basis.

Figure 3.1. **The Impacts of Trade Policies on the Spatial Deployment of a Firm's Value-chain**

| | Marketing | Assembly | Parts Production | R&D | Regional Co-ordination |
|---|---|---|---|---|---|
| Regional Economic Integration | | | | | ▓ |
| Technical Trade Barriers, Protective IPR policy | | | | ▓ | |
| Local Content Rules | | | ▓ | | |
| Contingent protection (Antidumping, Countervailing duty) | | ▓ | | | |
| Effective Standard Protection | | ▓ | | | |
| No Effective Trade Barriers | ▓ | | | | |

*Note:*    Shaded areas represent segments of a firm's value-chain most likely to be shifted in response to host-country trade policies listed on the left.

Absent trade barriers, the optimal shape of the value chain's spatial distribution would be concave, as represented in Figure 2.3; downstream activities would be decentralised while upstream activities would remain more centralised. Restrictive trade policies, however, would change this to a convex shape. As discussed in Chapter 2, globalisation is a process in which firms construct the optimal facility location for global profit maximisation. Trade barriers distort these optimal locational patterns because they prevent firms from taking full advantage of differences in production costs among locations and exploiting economies of scale and scope.

Optimally, for example, R&D can be performed on a global scale while core parts production can operate on a global or intermediate scale. Restrictive trade policies lead those functions to be deployed regionally or nationally, such that their scale economies cannot be fully exploited. Some Korean electronics firms distribute their core parts production in many regions, with most of the operations at far below the optimum. They have distributed their value chains to meet arbitrary government interventions such as local–content rules, which distort the optimal location of value–added activities and waste resources.

The effect of restrictive trade policy differs not only across the value chain but also across more and less vulnerable products. There can be many reasons, but a major one lies in the industrial incidence of trade policies. Importing countries try hardest to protect declining industries and targeted or "strategic" industries that they want to promote. Many developed countries maintain trade policies protecting some labour–intensive industries — which often are not sustainable over time even with protection, so that domestic firms withdraw and the protection is removed or bargained away in trade negotiations.

The United States, for instance, invoked contingent protection for colour television producers in the 1980s. By the early 1990s, all US local firms had withdrawn from many consumer electronics industries, including CTVs and VCRs. The US government has since seldom sought recourse to trade action against imports of those products. In the EU, on the other hand, some domestic firms remain in those industries. Korean business people in the EU interviewed by the author expect that domestic EU firms will withdraw from the industry sooner or later. Host countries obviously lose interest in using restrictive trade policy when there is no domestic industry to protect. This can have significant spatial effects. If firms invest only to circumvent trade barriers, they may have no reason to locate production there.

Countries select industries as strategic on considerations of technology and industrial development. Most countries consider electronic switches, integrated circuits and other technology–intensive telecommunication equipment as key industries and thus have some promotion policies including import restrictions, technical barriers, and government–procurement preferences. The rationale behind such protection is that those industries have high externality effects on technology and industrial development. Key industries are more frequently subject to restrictive trade policies than others.

When restrictive trade measures take effect, some products become more responsive to differentiated markets. As a result, differences in market responsiveness across products become less noticeable than when such measures are not present. For instance, geographical proximity to the market is, in principle, less critical for DRAMs and CPTs than for personal computers, TVs and VTRs. Restrictive trade measures such as local–content rules or restrictive IPR policies blur these distinctions as they make even DRAMs and CPTs more responsive to local markets.

Recently, Korean enterprises have been compelled to set up manufacturing subsidiaries for industries in which they are still strengthening competitive advantages in trade by building up their ownership of advanced technology. Most Korean investment in CPTs, integrated circuits, electronic switches and other technology–intensive telecommunication equipment may be partially triggered by restrictive trade policies. Those products are often subject to trade disputes. There is an argument that NTBs tend to be applied most heavily on products in which the developing countries have established or are establishing comparative advantage (Yeats, 1979).

To sum up: government regulations can exert influence over firms' locational decisions and thus have significant effects on the spatial distribution of the value chain. When host governments provide incentives to attract FDI, the effects on FDI are direct. Protective trade policies, however, have indirect effects, which supports the argument that trade protection can substitute for fiscal and financial incentives in attracting FDI inflows. Some critics even insist that trade policy is likely to have a more significant impact than investment policy itself because the fear of protective policies will accelerate FDI flows to avoid market insecurity (Han, 1992). Several empirical studies support those arguments. Barrell and Pain (1993) found that Japanese FDI during 1980s was significantly influenced by trade–protection measures, especially successful antidumping cases.

Other studies maintain that incentives to attract FDI do not have a significant impact on the total amount of FDI outflow from firms, but affect only the location of investment. Therefore, competition to attract investment is like a beggar–thy–neighbour policy. This suggests that governments should focus on developing incentive policies that do not distort location decisions. Hurter and Martinich (1989) assert that policies intended not to affect such decisions by firms may still have a significant spatial effect. They further insist that locational incentives can be designed to be mutually beneficial to both governments and firms *vis–à–vis* tradtional policies.

# Notes

1.   Helpman and Krugman (1985) insist that single plants can arise to exploit factor–cost differentials fully.

2.   The definition of acceptable injury "thresholds" is a thorny and controversial subject.

*Chapter 4*

# Changing Production Technology and Global Deployment of the Value Chain

## The Evolution of Production Technologies

Restrictive trade measures are not the only external factors that can change the optimal deployment of a firm's value chain based on factor proportions. New production technologies may also have effects because they can change factor intensity. To uncover the relationship between production technologies and the spatial distribution of a firm's value chain abroad, this chapter begins with a review of the literature on production systems[1]. It then suggests the most feasible and likely spatial distribution of their value chains by firms employing new production technologies and discusses whether this concept can be extended to investment by developing country firms.

The evolution of production systems traces back to the craft, later assisted by machine tools invented in the United Kingdom and United States in the 1800s. "Scientific" management, introduced by Taylor around 1900 in the United States, led to a surge in output growth. It had a fundamental impact on production, and massive changes took place in all manufacturing sectors. Its basic concept was very simple: the more specialised and divided are production activities, the greater will productivity increases be. The assembly line developed by Ford in the United States reinvigorated scientific management in work organisation. It refined the concept, assigning very limited and specialised tasks to workers so that even those with low or no skills could efficiently fulfil their tasks in mass assembly.

Mass production of standardised goods developed, with two intrinsic constraints according to Boyer (1993). First, firms had to secure large, stable and if possible increasing markets in order to ensure operation of the assembly–line process. Second, high capital/output ratios implied high break–even points and increasing returns to scale, which limited the application of typical mass–production systems to highly differentiated and segmented products and markets. Because of these characteristics, the typical system was challenged in various ways. The initiative came from workers, at first in the car industry at the end of the 1960s. Low–skilled blue–collar workers revolted against their simple and boring tasks, and trade unions struck. Fundamentally, better–educated generations rejected the basic axioms of mass production, and shortages of workers emerged in some industrialised countries.

Firms tried unsuccessfully to push mechanisation ahead. Instead, and especially in most OECD countries, productivity slowed in growth and even declined, notably in 1974–75 (Glyn, 1990). Changing consumption patterns also undermined the system. As disposable incomes increased with continuous economic growth, consumers became more sensitive to product quality and differentiation, demanding more diversified, higher quality and unique products. The mass–production system, with its rigid nature and inertia, could not satisfy these sophisticated consumers. Rearranging large assembly lines for model changes generally was expensive and involved time–lags.

Worldwide competition progressively destabilised oligopolistic competition based on mass production. In the fast expansion of trade during the last several decades, improved production systems outperformed typical mass production (Boyer, 1993). As many producers entered export markets with better systems, firms found it necessary to alter their previous patterns of production organisation to achieve higher quality levels and lower production costs simultaneously — and to meet changing market needs for greater customisation of finished products[2]. In response to these challenges, some innovative firms had struggled to develop better production systems ever since the 1950s. Until the 1970s, their efforts were mostly trial–and–error, and they improved productivity and flexibility only marginally.

Advances in electronic controlling technology followed by the introduction of computer numerical control in the mid–1960s brought about more fundamental changes. This technical innovation has developed along the whole process of operations from design and testing to fabrication, assembly, quality control, storage and delivery. Programmable, multitask equipment enables firms to produce a variety of outputs without rearranging manufacturing facilities. Computerised order processing allows firms to apply "just–in–time" deliveries of necessary inputs, which dramatically reduce inventories of components and final goods. Firms can integrate such new technologies through the application of electronic data communications.

Such technical innovation, although it is the most common element of the new system, is only one aspect of a whole spectrum of innovation. Great flexibility in the numbers of employees and working hours, along with functional flexibility in jobs, reveals another aspect. Innovations have centred especially on the improvement of work flexibility, which requires collaborative management–worker relations and a multi–skilled workforce. It can be an alternative to mechanisation. In some cases, multi–skilled workers can replace heavy mechanisation[3]. The new system thus has been accompanied by radical changes not only in mechanical facilities but also in the nature of work and its organisation.

Individual firms, for the most part, have developed or improved the new production system, through a long evolutionary process in which innovations have spread from first–mover firms to others in the developed countries and further to some firms in developing countries. Firms persistently search for effective and optimal operating models. Consequently, they have introduced many new organisational forms, including infinitely flat organisations, spider–web organisations, the cluster forms and federated enterprises. These have their own unique features but share basic common characteristics in moving toward a new flexible, flat and dynamic techno–organisational paradigm. Because of its evolutionary nature, the system is still considered experimental, even in developed countries (OECD, 1991*b*).

As this new system evolved in various manifestations of technical and organisational innovation, it had further impacts on management, including basic principles, organisation structure and information flow. Emerging management modes vary from firm to firm, from industry to industry and from country to country. Yet both the old and the new systems deal with common structural elements that permit some comparison between them. Table 4.1 shows the striking contrast between the two systems. The strength of flexible production lies in its capacity to manufacture relatively small volumes of goods cheaply. Mass production required machines dedicated to a single task. They had to be either rebuilt or replaced to change a product. Flexible production, however, brings a high degree of diversity without physically rearranging manufacturing facilities. Different products can be made on the same line with marginal additional cost. Under hard automation the greatest economies came only with massive output, but flexible production can yield similar economies with a wide range of products made in small batches (Bylinsky, 1983).

Table 4.1. **Comparison of the Mass Production and Flexible Production Systems**

|  | Mass Production System | Flexible Production System |
|---|---|---|
| Principle | Producer–oriented manufacturing | Customer–oriented, knowledge–intensive value–added activities |
| Organisation structure | Vertical (Tree structure) | Horizontal (Network structure) |
| Information flow | One–way (Order–obedience) | Multi–path (persuasion–consent) |
| Origin of value creation | Capital goods | Information + human capital |
| Production structure | Rigid | Flexible |
| Spectrum of products | Single | Numerous |
| Source of competitiveness | Low–cost, Based on economies of scale | High consumer responsiveness with reasonable price, based on economies of scale |

*Source:*    Based on concepts in Boyer (1993) as modified by the author.

Besides such product diversification, numerous other benefits are possible. The OECD (1991*b*) listed the most frequently cited motives for applying flexible production systems as follows:

— Improving product quality;

— Increasing production efficiency and flexibility of labour and equipment;

— Reducing lead times;

— Better control of production and technological capabilities (reliability, unsupervised production, organisation advantages); and

— Reducing production costs by decreasing labour costs.

Some of these benefits are easily measured, especially the reduction of labour cost. In fact this and, more broadly, lower production costs and improved productivity are the most commonly cited motives. Yet the more important real benefits are improved quality, faster times and better relations with suppliers and customers. They tend to be intangible and often more complicated and less easily estimated in advance. Several studies confirm that intangible benefits such as increased flexibility and customer responsiveness, better quality control and improved supplier links are often more important, but they are too difficult to quantify. The application of the new system nevertheless can still be justified on the basis of more quantifiable criteria such as labour saving (OECD, 1991*b*).

In short, the flexible production system has allowed small–batch production and shortened production cycles. This in turn has enabled firms to respond to changing market demand. At the organisational level, firms are becoming much more innovative, logistics–managing and customer–oriented entities. They focus on the development of critical and unique core competencies — unique technologies, knowledge bases, skills, databases and organisational motivation systems. Based on these core competencies, they can rapidly switch from one set of activities to another. They thus can move rapidly in and out of regional market niches with smaller, specialised plants for small–batch outputs (Storper, 1992).

## Flexible Production and the Spatial Deployment of a Firm's Value Chain

With flexible production, labour costs become less important in total production costs. This makes factor intensity less critical in determining the spatial distribution of the value chain. This might have an impact on the distribution of traditionally labour–intensive activities such as assembly. It may also change the importance of scale economies. In the old system, firms depended on mass production to exploit scale economies. In the new one, they can make use of advantages derived from economies of both scale and scope. In fact, some firms adopting the new system have successfully increased their production volume while at the same time increasing the range of models produced with the same equipment (OECD, 1991$b$). The impact of the new system on economies of scale is mixed and different from industry to industry and from firm to firm. One study found that plant size became smaller (Sengenberger and Loveman, 1987).

The most important aspect of the new system is that it intrinsically requires physical proximity not only between producers and their parts suppliers but also producers and consumers. One of its key competitive strengths lies in eliminating the sizeable financial cost of carrying large inventories of inputs and outputs. Physical proximity to suppliers and consumers is essential to take advantage of this. The new system demands a flow of inputs fully co–ordinated in line with the just–in–time principle. It can reduce costs substantially and even create some synergistic effects, but given its complexity it is relatively vulnerable if input supply does not function well (Oman, 1994).

The importance of proximity between producers and suppliers has in turn affected sourcing patterns. Global firms can source inputs from countries where the production cost of each part is the lowest. Such global sourcing scatters suppliers. Yet just–in–time production systems require tight control of parts supply because timely delivery of inputs is critical. Firms adopting the new system thus favour national or sub–national over inter–country and inter–regional sourcing. Although many firms tend to externalise the production of parts and components to avoid being locked in heavy investments, some are inclined to become further involved in core–parts production to ensure stable supply and avoid its control by others. This constitutes one of the key elements driving international vertical integration.

This study has maintained that firms can achieve global efficiency by distributing their value chains in different places. The benefits of global efficiency come not only from such optimal distribution but also from its linkage or synergy effects. The new production system in fact depends more on synergy effects than on efficiency derived from optimal location. Those effects can be generated more easily with geographical proximity among the segments of the value chain. Therefore, firms applying the new production system tend to gather more segments of the value chain in the target market in order to benefit from them.

Proximity to customers, another critical aspect of the system, provides two–way information flows that allow producers to adapt quickly to changing market demand and consumer preferences. In the mass–production system, firms tried to sell products after they were developed and produced. Therefore, customer response to new products could be obtained only after the completion of product development, and the process often became expensive. In the new system, however, firms seek a two–way flow of communication between final users and designers to reduce the risk of failures. This is especially critical for sophisticated equipment and consumer durables. In industries such as computers, the needs and proposals of final users provide a large source of innovation. Closeness and links between final users and designers are essential in the software industry (Boyer, 1993).

Figure 4.1 shows how the spatial–distribution contour changes with flexible production. The initial contour, which reflected only differences in factor intensity across the value chain, was concave. Artificial interventions such as trade barriers made it convex, indicating that midstream and upstream activities need to be more sensitive to market proximity. Introducing flexible production has further reduced the economic scale of all functions, including upstream and midstream activities, although substantial differences in economic scale remain size across the value chain.

Figure 4.1. **Changed Contour for the Spatial Distribution of Value-chain with Flexible Production**

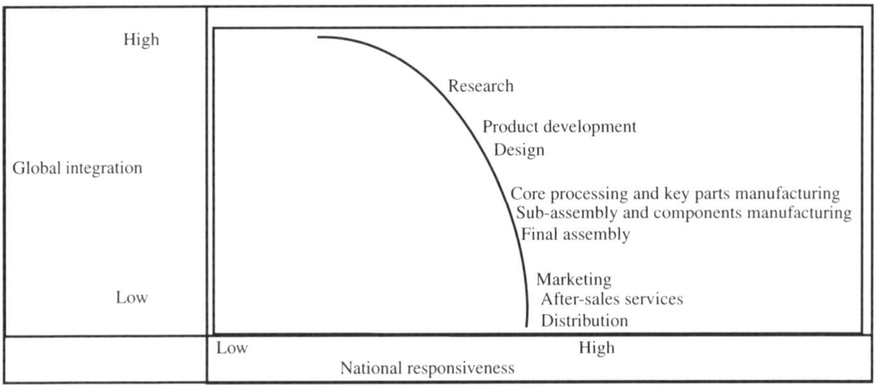

*Source:* Same as Figure 2.3.

As firms increasingly adopt the new production technology in the whole operational process, from design and testing to fabrication, assembly, quality control, storage and delivery, all segments of the value chain can become more responsive to national or regional differentiation. Not only assembly but also parts production and design are inclined to shift more to the target markets. Figure 4.2 illustrates this, as all functional activities shift downward and to the right. The figure shows that products such as CPTs would be more responsive to differentiated markets with the application of new system, although CPTs and ICs do not need market proximity as much as personal computers, TVs and VCRs. Marketing and after–sales services must be closer to the market than parts production and R&D. The right–hand diagram of the figure nevertheless indicates that most upstream and midstream functions for consumer electronics should shift downward and to the right. The introduction of the new, flexible system has led differences in market responsiveness across products and functions to become less noticeable.

Figure 4.2. **Changed Contour for the Deployment of the Firm's Value-chain with Flexible Production**

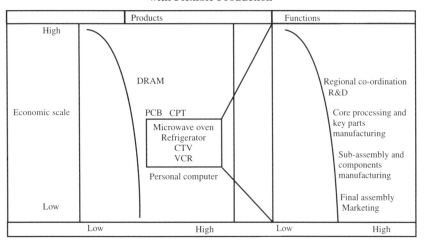

*Source:* Same as Figure 2.3.

Considerable differences exist across countries in the density of applying new production systems. From a survey of industrialised countries, the OECD concluded that the new system suits products using established technology and demanding substantial assembly (OECD, 1991*b*). Some consumer electronics products therefore have high potential to apply the new system. TVs and VCRs, for example, have well–established technology and considerable assembly. In fact, the electronics industry has come increasingly to apply the system for small–batch production of such items to meet differentiated market demand.

The extent of the system's application varies across industries. Some sectors have played a leading role in spreading it in many industrialised countries. The stock of installed micro–electronic equipment is highly concentrated in a few industrial sectors. Industrial robots have more limited use in sectors such as automobiles and electronics. The OECD found that these two sectors have more than half of the total stock of industrial robots in most industrialised countries (OECD, 1991*b*).

## Application of Different Production Technologies by Developing Country Firms

Advanced production technology is generally suitable for flexible production in certain circumstances but not in others; no single system suits all firms or all locations. The extent of application of the new system depends on a firm's strategy and locational factors, as well as on managerial skills and technological levels. The locational factors include related technology and industry development, flexibility in labour relations, and social infrastructure (Hirst and Zeitlin, 1991). The flexible production system cannot fully replace mass production. Both systems currently coexist in global production, with many hybrid forms of flexible specialisation, mass production or a combination of both.

The availability of different production systems has enabled firms to produce abroad with different technologies in different regions. Some firms have accumulated the whole spectrum of production technology from rigid to flexible. They can produce globally with the most suitable production technologies for each location. They may deploy outdated production facilities and technologies in developing countries while establishing new facilities and technologies at home or in more advanced countries.

The new system is not applicable under certain constraints, such as shortages of trained labour, a lack of software development and/or weaknesses in transportation and communications infrastructure. Poor infrastructure, including telecommunications networks, presents one of the most critical problems for developing countries in adopting the new production system. In addition to the physical constraints, developing countries are at a disadvantage in terms of the quantity and quality of human resource development. These locational constraints have produced wide dispersion across countries in the application of the new production system (OECD, 1991*b*).

Besides these external constraints, developing country firms are often limited in the application of the new production system because of their managerial and technological limitations. Developing country firms need to absorb and digest foreign–developed production technology before applying it to their own foreign manufacturing. To avoid the high risks, they likely will apply production technologies with which they are experienced and familiar in domestic production.

Most developing country firms therefore are likely to engage in foreign production with less sophisticated technology in other developing countries. Many Korean firms, however, have invested in developed as well as developing countries, as discussed earlier. Some Korean electronics conglomerates have established global production networks organised primarily on a regional basis, with networks of production complexes in each of the world's major markets such as Europe, North America, ASEAN and China. Two questions arise. What makes Korean firms show a unique investment pattern for global production, and will their investment grow and be commercially viable over the long run? To answer these questions, one must consider all the locational, technological and trade–policy factors together, which is the task of Chapter 5.

# Notes

1.  The new production systems of recent years encompass a rather wide spectrum of changes, which their names reflect — lean production, advanced manufacturing technology or flexible production, depending on their main emphasis. The notion of flexible production systems most comprehensively captures the human dimension.

2.  Customisation means manufacturing a product or delivering a service in response to a particular customer's needs.

3.  For instance, NEC, a Japanese electronics company already locked into heavy investment for factory automation, developed a new teamwork system for final assembly by hand to produce mobile phones. A team of 3–4 workers performed final assembly initially done by machine. With such teamwork, the company has successfully responded to changing demand while avoiding additional investment for model changes. This is often called the "spider–web" organisational form.

# Chapter 5

# Investment Modes for the Globalisation of Developing Country Firms

## Introduction

Chapter 2 concluded that downstream activities tend to be more decentralised than upstream activities, because they are relatively small and need consumer proximity. Upstream activities are big and need less such proximity. Chapter 3 argued that restrictive trade policy in host countries can change this value chain configuration, because exporting firms respond to it by shifting functions (e.g. assembly and parts production) to target markets. Chapter 4 contended that the application of new production technologies could further modify the configuration of the value chain, if factor intensity and the need for market proximity change as production technologies evolve.

This analysis dealt only with the partial impact of individual factors. Yet, in reality, these factors affect the spatial distribution of the value chain simultaneously as they interact to produce favourable or unfavourable conditions for a firm's decision–making. The necessary integration of those partial effects is a complicated task because the factors are not static but change over time. Factor costs and their compatibility with new production technology change with infrastructure construction and the education and training of work forces. A firm's competitive advantages also shift as it accumulates technological and managerial know–how. Because firms distribute their value chains, through FDI, in response to changing production technology and environments in home and host countries, FDI should be understood as a dynamic phenomenon.

Several studies explain firms' dynamic responses to changing technological and competitive environments (see, for example, Kogut, 1985 and Mucchielli, 1992). They develop their arguments by explaining firms' strategic responses to different combinations of competitive and comparative advantages, which correspond to ownership and locational advantages. This chapter develops a modified framework based on these studies to explain the recent investment patterns of firms based in NIEs. It then classifies FDI into several categories and discusses their different characteristics.

## Possible Investment Modes of Developing Country Firms

Kogut (1985) and Mucchielli (1992) maintain that, given their competitive advantages, firms are most likely to change their international operations in response to the changing comparative advantage of their home countries. Similarly, given that comparative advantage, they will move as their competitive advantages change. As argued in the previous chapter, when firms accumulate production technologies, they can shift their production locations or apply their different production technologies in response to the changing comparative advantages of their home countries. Furthermore, some developing country firms invest abroad not just to exploit but to improve their competitive advantages.

Market factors in host countries induce many investments not consistent with these arguments. For instance, developing country firms move out of the export mode in response to tariff and non–tariff barriers in major markets. The interplay of many factors creates complexity in suggesting prevailing modes of penetration. It also implies that FDI for the globalisation of developing country firms is not homogenous. Therefore, the determinants of FDI can hardly be generalised, because of the complex interactions among three sets of factors: comparative advantages of home countries, market factors in host countries and competitive advantages of investing firms.

Nevertheless, certain kinds of FDI from developing countries may have common factors. It might be useful to classify FDI into several types in order to identify them. This will reveal different policy implications and further suggest more desirable national and international policies. Some simplifications will help the classification. First, assume that competitive advantage refers to the production technology of investing firms, and that comparative advantage represents the compatibility of location with new production technology. Suppose further that home countries have become NIEs rather than developing countries, with competitive strengths in the electronics industry in the world market. In the NIEs, some firms will have enhanced their production technology while others will have failed to do so. In extreme cases, firms can develop production technology too sophisticated to be applied in their home countries.

Based on this analytical setting, Figure 5.1 schematises the prevailing FDI modes for each combination of three factors: the home and host countries' development levels and firms' production technology. Firms tend to improve their technology in parallel with the economic development of their home countries. The thick vertical arrow from cell (2.3) to cell (3.3) indicates this, while the thick horizontal arrow from cell (2.2) to cell (2.3) indicates the home country's shift from developing country to NIE status. At the individual firm level, however, technology development does not necessarily advance in parallel with the economic development of the home country. Some firms may improve their production technology more slowly than average or, in exceptional cases, very little. Firms that improve their production technologies too slowly cannot remain competitive because of changed factor costs in their home countries. For them, the prevailing mode of international operation is to shift conventional production to developing countries, a form of delocalisation. Cells (1.1) and (1.2) represent these

Figure 5.1. **The Possible Investment Modes of Developing Country Firms**

| Competitive advantages of firms (production system) | | | | | |
|---|---|---|---|---|---|
| High | Flexible production system | (4.1) | (4.2) | (4.3) | *Vertical integration, -High tech. parts - R & D*<br><br>Horizontal expansion -Assembly - *Key Parts* (4.4) |
| Medium | Mixed production system | Horizontal expansion -Assembly<br>*-Some competitive parts (3.1)* | Horizontal expansion -Assembly<br>*-Some competitive parts (3.2)* | Horizontal expansion -Assembly<br>*-Some competitive parts (3.3)* | *Vertical integration -R&D, design*<br>Horizontal expansion -Assembly<br>*-Some competitive parts (3.4)* |
| | | Horizontal expansion -Assembly<br>*-Some competitive parts (2.1)* | (Home)<br>Horizontal expansion -Assembly<br>(Firm)<br>*-Some competitive parts (2.2)* | Horizontal expansion -Assembly<br>*-Some competitive parts (2.3)* | Horizontal expansion -Assembly<br>*-Some competitive parts (2.4)* |
| Low | Mass production system | Delocalisation -Assembly -Common parts | Delocalisation -Assembly -Common parts | | |
| | | *Vertical integration -Labour intensive parts (1.1)* | *Vertical integration -Labour intensive parts (1.2)* | (1.3) | (1.4) |
| | | Least developing country | Developing country | NIEs/ (Home) | Developed country |
| | Comparative advantages of countries | | | | |
| | Low ←——— Medium ———→ High<br>(K/L endowment, infrastructure, trade policy) | | | | |

*Note:* The shading of each cell represents the degree of economic rationale of concerned investment.

types of FDI. Assembly and common parts manufacturing are the activities most likely to move because of their labour intensity and need for market proximity. Some Korean FDI in textiles and footwear in developing countries (e.g. South Asia), especially by small and medium–sized companies, might fall under this category. Labour–intensive production technology and low labour costs constitute major sources of competitiveness for these types of FDI.

Firms most commonly improve their technology incrementally and apply the familiar technology of domestic production to foreign production. They can install new facilities and apply incrementally improved technology at home while moving old facilities to developing countries to exploit the familiar technology there, beginning with assembly. This increases revenues and net profits. Cell (2.2) represents this type of FDI.

Some theorists use this argument to explain FDI from developing countries to other developing countries (e.g. Lall, 1983; Wells, 1983). Most Korean FDI in developing countries such as ASEAN falls into this category. Its competitiveness relies on familiar production technology and abundant semi–skilled workers in local markets.

In contrast, other firms may be able to enhance their production technologies faster than the development of their home countries. The new production technologies require fulfilment of several preconditions, including adequately skilled labour, microelectronics and related software, supporting industries and infrastructure. Owing to shortfalls in these prerequisite conditions, some leading firms in NIEs cannot apply at home production technologies that they have developed. A response can be the establishment of new production in more developed countries, with facilities applying less sophisticated technologies most likely maintained in the home countries. With this type of FDI, firms can accumulate production technology through learning by doing. For this reason, they may invest regardless of commercial viability. The newly developed and assimilated technology can be used or transferred to parents or other subsidiaries. Horizontal expansion in cell (4.4) might include FDI of this type. An example could be semiconductor manufacturing by leading Korean conglomerates in the United States and the EU.

FDI can occur either to exploit existing competitive advantage (production technology) or to strengthen it. NIE firms are rather weak in R&D and design. They can invest in developed countries to complement these weaknesses. The vertical integration in cells (4.4) and (3.4) represents this type of FDI. As the notion of integration implies, these investments will extend and internalise R&D, design and higher–technology parts production. Some FDI by Korean electronics firms to establish research labs or design centres in developed countries falls into this category.

NIE firms can also invest in developing countries for vertical integration. Some rely on supplies of low–cost, labour–intensive parts from the developing countries and the least developing countries. MNCs based in developed countries often use global subcontracting and outsourcing strategies for cheaper supplies of such parts or products. Most NIE firms do not have equivalent bargaining powers or techniques, but are more familiar with labour–intensive production technologies. Therefore, they have motives to produce those parts in developing countries themselves, not only for timely supply but also for better quality control. Vertical integration in cells (1.1) and (1.2) represents this kind of investment, which includes some investments by the Korean electronics industry in least developed and developing countries for offshore production of common parts.

The discussion so far has focused on FDI whose purpose is not only to respond to the discordance between firms' existing production technology and production conditions in home countries but also to complement, through vertical integration, weak segments of their value chains. Firms can invest abroad without such motives, however. A more common type might be FDI with the same production technology as at home, regardless of locational differences in host countries. The main motive would be market proximity. Firms can choose direct investment over export when the advantages of proximity overwhelm the costs associated with using production technology less suited to the host country. The same proximity rationale applies in cases where firms maintain in home operations both familiar and somewhat more advanced production technologies. Even if the latter have not yet improved enough for them to be involved in fully efficient developed–country production, the investments may go ahead when the benefits of market proximity outweigh the costs of production inefficiency. To minimise efficiency losses, firms tend to operate assembly functions only. Horizontal expansion in cell (3.4) represents this type of FDI, which may include a substantial portion of Korean investments in developed countries.

Some firms invest in developing countries even though their technologies are too sophisticated for them, so that production in developing countries is more expensive than at home. Market proximity once again provides the rationale. Horizontal expansion in cell (3.2) represents this type of FDI, which includes some Korean FDI for car manufacturing in developing countries.

Another type of FDI has no apparent economic rationale. Why do some firms invest in developed countries with outdated production technology while others invest in developing countries with too–advanced technology — even when the advantage of market proximity cannot justify the costs? Horizontal expansion in cells (2.4) and (3.1) represents the former and the latter respectively. Policy–induced distortions provide the answer in both cases.

Firms are forced to invest in developed countries such as the United States and the EU — cell (2.4) — when their market security there is threatened. Consumer–electronics industries are heavily scale–intensive, and most domestic NIE markets are relatively small compared with the required economic size. Therefore, firms have relied heavily on major export markets, especially the established ones. Yet contingent trade–policy actions, notably antidumping charges, have often threatened that market security. In such circumstances, investment in assembly has been the response, to maintain market share.

The main reason behind horizontal expansion to developing countries, as in cell (3.1), might also involve limitations on market access, often through standard protection. Because the market potential in many of these markets is increasing, many leading firms try to establish market platforms there. When market access is limited, establishing only marketing subsidiaries would contribute little. The most common way to circumvent the trade barriers is to establish assembly subsidiaries regardless of profitability in the short run. To reduce losses, firms try to maintain minimum final–assembly functions and to import parts as semi–assembled kits as much as possible. Some automobile investments in least developing countries exemplify this category.

Figure 5.1 indicates that the distribution of assembly functions mostly characterises FDI for horizontal expansion. Since the main motive is market proximity, firms tend to debundle remaining functions and locate them at home or elsewhere abroad. This often conflicts with the host countries' trade policies. Some developing countries impose local–content requirements as a condition for approval of investments, making investment in parts production mandatory. Many developed countries also have local–content regulations. They exert a strong influence over the distribution of the value chains of investing firms, including shifts of some competitive parts production.

## Different Types and Characteristics of FDI

Figure 5.1 suggests new taxonomic criteria for the classification of FDI. One can select numerous such criteria, depending on the purposes of the classification. In line with the main themes of this book — to discover why developing country firms deploy various functions across different regions and what impact FDI has on exports from the home country — it is useful to classify FDI by criteria that study firms' motives for FDI projects and what kinds of functions they distribute abroad through FDI. Horizontal and vertical integration constitute the main motives for FDI in this scheme.

Firms use horizontal integration to take advantage of market proximity and economies of scale, especially at the firm level. In contrast, they seek vertical integration to exploit differences in factor cost and in plant and firm economies of scale. Horizontal integration can be further classified into offensive (voluntary) and defensive (non-voluntary) integration, depending on whether FDI results from deliberate rationalisation strategy or is an inevitable response to internal or external challenges. Delocalisation, a fourth category, refers to a redeployment of production facilities abroad accompanied by a closure of domestic facilities.

Table 5.1 highlights this categorisation. The first column lists the four categories of FDI and the fourth characterises each category by purpose and function. The second shows the cells in Figure 5.1 that fall under each category. The third classifies the different functions performed in more detail. The classification scheme can be further disaggregated or aggregated depending on the purposes of analysis.

Because factor intensity and the need for market proximity differ across different functions of firms, firms have different motives in distributing their functions, through FDI, in distant countries. By the same logic, they also have different motives, across the four different types of FDI, in making decisions to invest abroad. Factor–price differences, which determine production costs, constitute the important motives for vertical integration, while various advantages derived from market proximity are more critical for horizontal integration.

Table 5.1. **Classification of FDI**

| Types of FDI | Corresponding Cells in Figure 5.1 | Performed Function | Corresponding Investments |
|---|---|---|---|
| Category I | Cell (4.4), (3.3), (2.2) | Assembly, high–tech. parts | Offensive horizontal expansion |
| Category II | Cell (3.2). (3.4). (2.1), (2.4), (3.1) | Assembly, parts | Defensive horizontal integration |
| Category III | Cell (1.1), (1.2), (3.4), (4.4) | R&D, high–tech. parts, labour–intensive parts | Vertical integration |
| Category IV | Cell (1.1). (1.2) | Assembly, common parts | Delocalisation |

A major motive behind FDI in category I is most likely to exploit market potential in the host country, while low host–country labour costs likely drive FDI in category IV. The defensive horizontal integration of category II occurs to circumvent trade barriers. When firms invest abroad for vertical integration (category III), they likely seek to acquire new technologies or deploy labour–intensive functions in developing countries. These major motives prescribe the most critical determinant factors for each type of FDI. Table 5.2 summarises the major characteristics and critical determinants of the different types of FDI.

The different characteristics of production technology and local markets set the different critical determinants of each type of FDI and suggest differences in economic rationale across the different types. The development paths of foreign subsidiaries depend on these differences. Against this background, one can look for deviations in development paths across different types of FDI.

The degree of shading in each cell in Figure 5.1 represents the degree of economic rationale for each type of investment, i.e. the level of commercial viability. For instance, horizontal expansion in cell (2.2) represents FDI with familiar production technology in less developed countries. It has an economic rationale and thus is lightly shaded. In contrast, horizontal expansion in cell (2.4) represents FDI with obsolete technology in developed countries. It has little economic rationale and is heavily shaded. Horizontal integration in cells (4.4), (3.3) and (2.2), vertical integration in cells (4.4), (3.4), (1.1) and (1.2) and delocalisation in cells (1.1) and (1.2) are not shaded because both factor–proportion and market–proximity hypotheses can explain them. Some horizontal integration, in cells (3.2), (2.1), and (3.4) has only light shading because factor–proportion arguments cannot satisfactorily explain it — but advantages derived from market proximity may compensate factor–cost disadvantages. Investments in the remaining cells, such as (3.1) and (2.4), cannot be justified in any economic sense and thus are darkly shaded. Disadvantages based on factor–proportion differentials would be too high to be compensated by advantages of market proximity. Such investments might most likely be forced by market threats.

Table 5.2. **Major Characteristics and Critical Determinants, by Different Types of FDI**

|  | Types of FDI | | | |
|  | Category I | Category II | Category III | Category IV |
|---|---|---|---|---|
| Local market characteristics | Increasing competitive pressure | Threatened | Increasing competitive pressure | Increasing competitive pressure |
| Major motives | Exploitation of marketing potential | Exhortations to increase output | Increasing fragmentation of process | Response to high domestic production cost |
| Distributed function | Extension of domestic operation | Extension of domestic operation | Acquisition of new function | Complete or partial domestic plant closure |
| Critical determinant factor of FDI | Magnitude of marketing potential | Threatening market security | Labour cost, technology bottleneck | Labour Cost |

Some horizontal expansion can be commercially viable under the condition that firms operate minimum final assembly activity in host countries and import parts in the form of semi–assembled kits as much as possible. Any forced relocation of parts production in response to host–country local–content regulation, however, would further deteriorate their profitability. The horizontal expansions in the heavily shaded cells (2.4) and (3.1) have little promise and can hardly survive.

As production technologies change, investing firms will try to adapt them to local markets. The small vertical arrows, i.e. those stretched from cell (2.3) to (3.3) and from (3.4) to (4.4), represent these changes. Viability will be enhanced as investments shift from shaded to non–shaded cells. Similarly, host countries' production conditions can improve. The small vertical arrows stretched from cells (3.1) to (3.2) and from cells (2.1) to (2.2) indicate the investment responses, as investors' firms improve their competitive positions. In fact, some firms may apply more advanced production systems with only the expectation of better production conditions in developing countries.

The types of FDI that have sufficient economic rationale would follow the sequential, evolutionary path described in Figure 2.5. Other types may have difficulty in following that path. To what extent, then, can this general framework explain the FDI development process adequately? This requires a closer look at the different categories of FDI.

Category I FDI (voluntary horizontal integration) — that in cells (4.4), (3.3) and (2.2) of Figure 5.1 — has a clear economic rationale and thus would most likely follow the sequence outlined in Figure 2.5. The difference between cell (4.4) and cells (3.3) and (2.2) lies in the establishment of R&D subsidiaries. FDI in cells (3.3) and (2.2) would skip that step and shift directly to regional headquarters because of limited availability of highly skilled scientists and engineers, and/or poor access to sources of basic scientific and technical developments (Behrman and Fisher, 1980). It is true that investing firms do not need to establish regional headquarters if market size cannot support several subsidiaries in a region. Major markets, however, including the EU, NAFTA, and China, have induced investing firms to establish high concentrations of regional headquarters because of their big domestic markets or regional economic integration.

Figure 5.2 shows the highly probable development paths of all four categories of FDI. They differ — and, because this is only a conceptually logical construct, real–world developments may also differ. Nevertheless, if investing firms can adapt successfully in host countries, Figure 5.2 approximates reality.

Figure 5.2. **Differences in the Sequential Process of Changing Entry Mode across Four Categories of FDI**

| Types of FDI | Possible Development Path of FDI | | |
|---|---|---|---|
| Category I | ① Marketing ⇒ | ② Local assembly ⇒<br>③ Manufacturing common parts ⇒<br>④ Manufacturing core parts ⇒ | ⑤ R&D ⇒<br>⑥ Regional integration |
| Category II | ① Marketing ⇒ | ② Local assembly ⇒<br>③ Manufacturing common parts | |
| Category III | | ① Manufacturing common parts ⇒<br>② Local assembly<br>② Manufacturing common parts | ⇐ ① R&D |
| Category IV | ② Marketing ⇐ ① Local assembly | ① Local assembly ⇒ | ② Manufacturing common parts |
| | Downstream | Midstream<br>Hierarchy of entry mode | Upstream |

Category II investments — in developing countries applying production technology too sophisticated for local markets, or in developed countries with technology not advanced enough for these markets — cannot develop far. Some investments may be narrowly viable as assembly subsidiaries supported by their parent companies. If forced by local–content rules to manufacture common parts, they can hardly survive and would retreat to the initial marketing mode.

Initial entry modes of FDI under category III (vertical integration) would be R&D subsidiaries or production subsidiaries for manufacturing common parts. They can develop toward lower modes. For example, R&D subsidiaries in developed countries for vertical integration may evolve production subsidiaries for some technology–intensive parts and components. Likewise, subsidiaries making common parts can be augmented with assembly plants to serve local markets. Although such developments might not be viable at first, the accumulation of host–country knowledge and linkage effects can make conditions favourable for them. A local assembly subsidiary is the likely initial entry mode of FDI under category IV. Firms invest to take advantage of low factor costs, especially for labour. Later development may go forward or backward, towards manufacturing common parts and/or towards marketing subsidiaries, because firms can benefit from both lower factor costs and market proximity.

# PART TWO

# THE DETERMINANTS OF FDI BY DEVELOPING COUNTRY FIRMS: EMPIRICAL ANALYSES

Part Two focuses on empirical evidence for the important arguments put forward in Part One. Chapter 6 presents a conceptual framework to explain the dynamic nature of FDI. It distinguishes foreign subsidiaries by entry modes. This places emphasis on factors affecting a firm's choice of an initial entry mode and later changes to other modes. Chapter 7 reports information collected from Korean electronics firms that can be used to verify hypotheses generated under this framework. It explores, for example, different determinants of entry modes across markets, firms, industries or products. This information also serves as the database for deeper empirical analysis in subsequent chapters, including those in Part Three.

To explain the dynamic aspects of FDI, one must extend or modify earlier models of the determinants of FDI. Working within the data constraints, Chapter 8 suggests and estimates a simple model to analyse the determinants in various ways and to verify the hypotheses. It covers the following related questions:

— What factors determine a firm's initial entry mode for a given product in a given market?

— What factors trigger a change from an initial mode to another one, again given the firm, the product and the market?

— What are the critical determinants for each type of FDI? If there is no consistency in determinants across different types of FDI, what are the major differences involved?

*Chapter 6*

# A Dynamic Framework for Investment Decision Making by Developing Country Firms

## Various Entry Modes

Firms establish foreign subsidiaries to distribute their activities in geographically different countries. The subsidiaries vary in the functions they perform, and thus can be classified into several modes: marketing, final assembly, sub–assembly and components manufacturing, core processing or key parts manufacturing, R&D and regional headquarters. The classification criteria are based on the typical divisions of a firm's value chain, as discussed in the preceding chapters. In practice, however, few subsidiaries perform these basic functions exclusively, which can blur the distinctions among them. Marketing subsidiaries might engage in some production. Final–assembly plants may do some components manufacturing. Sub–assembly and components manufacturing subsidiaries can perform R&D. Higher–level units may carry out the functions of lower–level ones. Assembly and components–manufacturing subsidiaries commonly also involve themselves in some marketing, and R&D subsidiaries as well as regional headquarters can also have production tasks.

The modal distinctions thus are somewhat arbitrary, but one still can distinguish units by the *major* functions they perform, which keeps the classification scheme useful as a basis for better understanding the dynamic nature of FDI. The key motivating factors remain operative. FDI for marketing is quite different from FDI for assembly. Firms establish assembly subsidiaries with different motives from those for components manufacturing and R&D. To make the distinctions clearer, the main activities of each mode need more extended discussion.

### Marketing Subsidiaries

These units do direct marketing and distribution of exported products to wholesalers and retailers in target markets. Firms use them to internalise these functions rather than rely on the external market, thus avoiding dependence on foreign buyers.

Establishing such subsidiaries enables investing firms to develop and market their own products, bringing to bear proprietary strengths based on their accumulated experience. They can be more responsive, not only in serving market needs with fast delivery and reliable after–sales services, but also in reflecting specific local needs. Developing country firms, especially, can escape from the original equipment manufacturer (OEM) trap and export under their own brand names.

### Final–Assembly Subsidiaries

Customers can perceive subsidiaries in this mode as representing a strong commitment to local markets because they necessarily involve the physical construction of factories. Because firms must transfer significant internal resources to establish these units, they generally make the investment only when the benefits possible from lower costs or market proximity can compensate the possible costs and risks. Nevertheless, some developing country firms have made final–assembly investments in developed countries to bypass trade barriers — but only when they were labour–intensive. Developing country firms that cannot apply advanced production technology suitable for developed countries may face difficulties if their subsidiaries face high labour costs.

### Sub–Assembly and Components–Manufacturing

In addition to simple "screwdriver" assembly plants, firms can shift some bulky parts manufacturing or sub–assembly to local markets, either to save transportation and acquisition costs or to meet local–content requirements. These activities can also be outsourced, but if that does not prove cost–effective, investing firms will establish these subsidiaries in host countries or ask their domestic subcontractors to invest in the region, near their assembly subsidiaries. Some Korean firms have recently shifted to or additionally established this mode in line with their localisation policies, and many domestic subcontractors have made such investments to serve their assemblers.

### Core Processing or Key Parts Manufacturing

Firms often must offset high labour costs in host countries by importing core parts from home. Core processing or key parts manufacturing usually concentrates in home countries. This often conflicts with host–country policy objectives to increase industrial value added within their territories as much as possible, often through strong local–content rules. Some investing firms may have only two options: either shift to manufacturing core parts in these countries or retreat to the marketing mode. Others, however, would perform this function in host countries to ensure stable input supplies or maintain the high quality of their products. The recent increase in the application of new production technologies also induces firms to shift this function to host countries.

### R&D Subsidiaries

In order to carry out more market–oriented strategies, firms need not only to be more sensitive to changes in local consumer tastes, but also to respond quickly to them. This has led firms to establish design centres and R&D institutes in target markets. In addition to this market–driven factor, developing country firms tend to establish abroad in this mode to supplement their weaknesses in R&D and design. They chiefly seek available, qualified labour in developed countries, because technology transfers through licensing or technology spillovers from FDI inflows often lag. Thus firms' functional motives for establishment abroad in this mode vary from product development or modification to localisation of design.

### *Regional Headquarters*

Headquarters subsidiaries perform a distinctive role. Their major responsibilities are to co–ordinate and control the activities of firms' regional affiliates. They can position firms better for the regional integration of marketing, finance, R&D, component manufacturing and assembly. The more subsidiaries a firm establishes, the more it needs to co–ordinate or integrate them. This mode is not exclusively for firms in developed countries. Korean electronics conglomerates have begun to establish regional headquarters in major markets. Some are already in operation in markets such as the EU and NAFTA, and some have set up or announced plans to establish new headquarters in ASEAN, China, India and Brazil.

## A Conceptual Framework for the Analysis of Dynamic Investment Decision Making

The decision to choose an entry mode requires a comprehensive evaluation of many factors (Root, 1986). Firms must consider not only economic but also organisational and strategic issues in the process of investment decision making. Some MNC studies (e.g. Bartlett and Ghosgal, 1989; Root, 1986) suggest numerous factors that exert influence on the choice of entry mode. Firms often evaluate them one by one, and the choice of an entry mode is a complicated procedure of trade–offs among alternatives. Some authors also note that productivity and flexibility can represent a trade–off; Bartlett (1984) cites a detergents company to support this.

Once decisions are made, changes in external or internal factors encourage or force firms to re–evaluate their previous entry modes and decide whether to move to higher modes or retreat to lower ones. External factors include both home and host–country factors. A more dynamic and comprehensive framework is necessary to understand how these changes happen. Figure 6.1 schematises it in the broadest context. Although a change of mode can be motivated by changes either in the external environment or in internal capabilities, it most likely results from the dynamic interaction of changes in both. The factors interact to make conditions favourable or unfavourable for each investment mode.

Under given conditions, firms may choose the "right" entry mode for certain target markets. Strategy and behaviour may differ across companies, however, even given the same conditions. A firm's final decision depends on its strategy for obtaining its specific objectives and its behaviour or attitude toward this strategy. Strategies or behaviour can thus become the ultimate influence determining investment under given internal and external factors. In other words, internal and external factors are necessary but not necessarily sufficient to determine modal choices.

As pointed out often in previous chapters, there is a sequence in changing entry modes. It implies that firms would shift to other entry modes based on their evaluation of the current ones, which serve as reference points for new investment decisions. If firms benefit from their current modes, they may continue to move to higher ones. This process is represented in Figure 6.1 by the arrows *a, b, c, d*. On the contrary, if firms do not so benefit, they may retreat to previous modes or withdraw from their international operations, as the arrows *e, f, g,* indicate.

This framework captures all of the important internal and external factors that affect entry modes, as well as firms' objectives, embodied in their strategies for growth through diversification. These elements, of course, do not necessarily play the same roles across the various categories of FDI delineated in Chapter 5. It remains now to discuss them briefly from a different point of view, namely the choice of variables to be used later in the analysis.

### *Internal Resources*

Firms' internal resources include management, capital, manpower, and production technology. The preceding chapters have maintained that firms can distribute their facilities more widely in developing and in developed countries as they accumulate more technology. They can choose higher entry modes when they have more internal resources in general, whereas limited or insufficient resources place constraints on choices of entry modes. Generally, the greater the internal resources in management, capital, technologies and production and marketing expertise that firms have, the greater the number of their entry modes, and *vice versa*.

Most developing country firms operate under the constraints of limited managerial, production, and marketing skills, but the level of these constraints does differ across firms, and some of them can overcome some of the constraints by investing abroad. Korean electronics firms diverge widely in managerial and technological capabilities, especially between small and medium enterprises (SMEs) and large conglomerates. Firms' internal capabilities include various elements, and many variables can represent them. Firm size and R&D intensity are the most frequently used variables in empirical analyses.

Figure 6.1. **Dynamic Framework for Investment Decision Making**

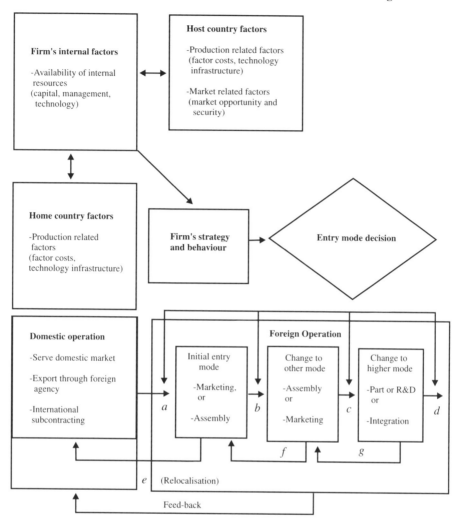

### Market–Related Factors

Most NIEs have relatively small domestic markets, and their exporting industries depend heavily on foreign markets, especially major ones such as the United States and the EU. Therefore, market threats from those countries become a matter of survival for them. Increasing protective measures, including antidumping, safeguards and voluntary export restrictions of developed countries, have led developing country firms to adopt defensive strategies. These strategies vary, depending on the magnitude of the stake involved and firms' available resources. If the stakes are large and a firm has the necessary internal financial and managerial resources, it can shift to local production to bypass the barriers and seek markets more aggressively.

New market opportunities represent another market–related factor affecting the investment decision. They arise from two sources. First, fast–growing local markets in some developing countries, especially in emerging Asian economies, offer significant and rapidly expanding market potential. Many of these countries maintain a policy mix of protective industrial and trade policies and promotional policies for FDI, which together induce foreign firms to commit to those markets. Second, new opportunities open up in markets that are expanding through regional economic integration. The most frequently cited variables used to represent market factors in empirical analyses are market size, market growth rates and trade policies of host countries.

### Production–Related Factors

*Ceteris paribus*, production and transport costs should determine the spatial distribution of industrial activities. Production costs in developing countries have changed rapidly. Firms will compare foreign and domestic production costs and, if the former are lower, may consider investment abroad after making cost comparisons for many locational candidates. Production cost is in fact the most critical locational determinant of FDI. In general, production costs depend on factor costs, namely labour and material costs. Because the electronics industry is not raw–materials intensive, labour costs dominate in its firms' consideration of many foreign projects.

As discussed in Chapter 4, however, the application of new production systems has made labour costs less important in total costs. Locational compatibility with new production technology, the technology infrastructure, has become a more important factor for some investments. Root (1986) mentions other variables affecting the choice of production sites, and it also is true that the importance of locational factors differs significantly across industries. Nevertheless, wage differentials and measures of technology infrastructure seem to be the most relevant variables explaining FDI in the electronics industry by developing country firms.

*Corporate Strategy and Behaviour*

In a market economy, firms exist to generate profits, and any firm that fails to do so over an extended period will inevitably go out of business. The pursuit of profit is a fundamental firm objective. To achieve it some firms focus on increasing market share while others stress short–term profits. Japanese firms once were characterised as having more interest in increasing market share. Korean firms also are more interested in increasing their size even if it results in sacrificing some short–term profits. Their growth patterns over two decades have a close relationship with this behavioural characteristic (Cho, 1983), and they consequently have been aggressive risk–takers in FDI.

Firms can grow through increasing the production or sales of a single product in a single plant. In the real world, however, they likely will grow through product and market diversification to take advantage of scope economies. Depending on a firm's strategy, diversification can proceed into other industries or into other markets. Some argue that the former is more difficult because technology and experience can be transferred more easily across markets than across industries (Lee, C. and Lee, K., 1991). For this reason, some developing country firms — including some Korean firms — follow a strategy of investing abroad to achieve their growth objectives. Nevertheless, firms do adopt different strategies under identical conditions among the other factors affecting investment decisions. This makes corporate strategy an independent factor. It also is a qualitative one, dependent primarily on management attitudes or organisational behaviour. Therefore, it is not easy to find quantitative variables to represent it, but economic concentration measures and the export ratios of investing firms can be used as variables indirectly related to product and market diversification.

*Chapter 7*

# Data and Analyses

## Data Source and the Sample

The main source of data for firm–specific factors in the empirical analyses here is the directory of Korean electronic firms engaging in overseas investment published by the Electronic Industries Association of Korea (EIAK). The EIAK instituted the Overseas Investment Council, whose members include most Korean electronics firms operating foreign subsidiaries. It conducts a survey biannually to collect basic data on foreign subsidiaries and their parent companies, and publishes the data as a directory. The directory includes data on the regional distribution of four different types of foreign affiliates: marketing subsidiaries, production subsidiaries, R&D subsidiaries and regional headquarters. In general, the most recent data used here are for 1996 or 1997.

The directory also provides some data on parent companies and their foreign subsidiaries. For parent companies, it covers their major products, the amount of capital, numbers of employees and sales and export volumes. Data on foreign subsidiaries differ depending on types of subsidiaries. For marketing affiliates, they cover the amount of capital, equity ratios, major products traded, numbers of employees and years of establishment and operation. The data for production subsidiaries indicate their major products, capital, equity ratios, numbers of employees, years of establishment and operation and major market and source countries. For R&D subsidiaries, some data on major research areas or products, numbers of researchers and establishment and operating years also are available. Data on regional headquarters include capital, equity ratios, numbers of employees, and establishment and operating years. Unfortunately, some data on some parent companies and their affiliates are missing. Those gaps were filled from other sources, such as financial reports on listed companies or direct telephone inquiries.

Although the directory provides a large amount of basic data, it does not include some statistics, such as R&D intensity of investing firms. This study also needed more disaggregated numbers on production, sales and exports of parent companies and their foreign subsidiaries. To collect them, a supplementary questionnaire was included in the EIAK's 1997 directory survey. It went to all member firms of the EIAK Overseas Investment Council. The questionnaire also collected some additional information, including locational data on host countries.

The sample consists of 66 parent companies and 361 subsidiaries. Among the parent companies, 13 are affiliates of the four biggest conglomerates. Nine others are large firms that have sales of more than $1 billion or belong to the 30 largest business groups. The remaining 44 firms are mostly small and medium–sized. Eleven parent companies are engaged in consumer electronics, with another 11 in industrial electronics. The majority, 44 parent firms, consists of component manufacturers. The four biggest Korean conglomerates have integrated vertically to dominate the domestic consumer electronics market. They have many affiliates manufacturing components. In contrast, other firms are mostly independent final–product or component manufacturers. The sectoral distribution of parent companies reflects these industrial characteristics (Table 7.1).

Table 7.1. **Parent Companies by Sector and Firm Size**

|  | Consumer Electronics | Parts & Components | Industrial Electronics | Total |
|---|---|---|---|---|
| Conglomerates | 3 | 8 | 2 | 13 |
| LEs | 5 | 2 | 2 | 9 |
| SMEs | 3 | 34 | 7 | 44 |
| **Total** | **11** | **44** | **11** | **66** |

*Note:* Conglomerates are the four biggest parent companies. LEs are large companies which have sales of more than $1 billion or belong to the 30 largest business groups. SMEs denote other parent firms.

Table 7.2 shows the number of foreign subsidiaries by parent–firm size. Conglomerates have established 238 foreign subsidiaries. SMEs have 84 and large companies the remaining 39. Overall, each parent company has established 5.47 subsidiaries on average, but there is disparity in the average number of subsidiaries per parent firm across firm sizes. Conglomerates have 18.3 subsidiaries per parent, while large companies have 4.3 and SMEs a minimal 1.9.

Table 7.2. **Foreign Subsidiaries by Parent–Firm Size**

|  | Marketing subsidiaries | Production subsidiaries | Research subsidiaries | Regional headquarters | Total |
|---|---|---|---|---|---|
| Conglomerates | 95 | 112 | 24 | 7 | 238 |
| LEs | 17 | 21 | 1 | 0 | 39 |
| SMEs | 29 | 55 | 0 | 0 | 84 |
| **Total** | **141** | **188** | **25** | **7** | **361** |

Variations also exist in subsidiaries across branches of the industry (Table 7.3). Conglomerates have established foreign subsidiaries mostly for consumer electronics, whereas the SMEs have focused their subsidiaries on manufacturing parts and components. Large companies have subsidiaries both for consumer electronics and for parts production. The average number of subsidiaries per parent company is highest in consumer electronics and lowest in parts and components.

Table 7.3. **Foreign Subsidiaries by Branch and Parent–Firm Size**

|  | Consumer electronics | Parts & components | Industrial electronics | Total |
|---|---|---|---|---|
| Conglomerates | 141 | 70 | 27 | 238 |
| LEs | 21 | 11 | 7 | 39 |
| SMEs | 3 | 63 | 18 | 84 |
| **Total** | **165** | **144** | **52** | **361** |

## Differences in Entry Modes

### *The Distribution of Entry Modes across Firms, Markets and Products*

Table 7.4 reveals differences in the distribution of entry modes across markets. In China and in ASEAN, Korean electronics industries have established more than 100 production subsidiaries but only around ten marketing subsidiaries. South Asia has no marketing subsidiaries at all. In contrast, Korean electronics firms operate more marketing than production subsidiaries in the EU and NAFTA, consistent with the common notion that the marketing function is more important in developed than in developing countries because of their relatively large market size and sophisticated consumer tastes. On the other hand, firms have a tendency to establish more production than marketing subsidiaries in developing countries to exploit factor–cost differentials between the home and host countries. All the research subsidiaries are in developed countries. Firms tend to establish R&D subsidiaries only in developed countries to exploit the high technological capabilities in those countries.

Table 7.4 .**Distribution of Entry Modes by Market**

|  | Marketing subsidiaries | Production subsidiaries | Research subsidiaries | Total |
|---|---|---|---|---|
| ASEAN | 11 | 45 | 0 | 56 |
| South Asia | 1 | 8 | 0 | 9 |
| China | 3 | 66 | 0 | 69 |
| NAFTA | 34 | 23 | 15 | 72 |
| EU | 32 | 28 | 3 | 63 |
| Others | 61 | 18 | 6 | 85 |
| **Total** | **142** | **188** | **24** | **354** |

*Note:* The number of regional headquarters is too small to be included.

One can construct a contingency table and use a chi–square test, a statistical significance test for categorical variables, to find whether differences in entry modes across markets are significant. The null hypothesis is that no difference exists in entry modes across markets[1]. To meet the basic requirement of the rule of five, Table 7.5 is a 2x3 contingency table. The $\chi^2$ value is 77.308, which far exceeds the critical value at the one per cent significance level (13.81). Therefore, the null hypothesis is rejected at the one per cent level. Highly significant differences exist in the distribution of entry modes across markets.

Table 7.5. **Contingency Table for Analysing the Relationship between Market and Type of Entry Mode**

|  | Marketing subsidiaries | Production subsidiaries | Research subsidiaries | Total |
|---|---|---|---|---|
| Developing countries | 15 | 119 | 0 | 134 |
| Developed countries | 66 | 51 | 18 | 135 |
| **Total** | **81** | **170** | **18** | **269** |

$\chi^2$ =77.308, contingency coefficient (cc) = 0.472, d.f. = 2

Differences in the distribution of entry modes across industry branches also are noticeable. The consumer electronics industry has a tendency to establish more marketing than production subsidiaries (Table 7.6). In contrast, the parts & components sub–sector tends to establish more production than marketing subsidiaries, while industrial electronics firms have established marketing and production subsidiaries almost equally. The industrial electronics sub–sector also has focused on establishing R&D subsidiaries. It has the biggest share of R&D subsidiaries, followed by parts and components and then consumer electronics.

Table 7.6. **Distribution of Entry Modes by Sector**

|  | Marketing subsidiaries | Production subsidiaries | Research subsidiaries | Total |
|---|---|---|---|---|
| Consumer electronics | 86 | 71 | 2 | 159 |
| Parts & components | 36 | 94 | 13 | 143 |
| Industrial electronics | 20 | 23 | 9 | 52 |
| **Total** | **142** | **188** | **24** | **354** |

Statistically highly significant differences also exist in the distribution of entry modes between finished and intermediate goods (Table 7.7). The null hypothesis is that there is no difference in entry modes across industries. Because consumer and industrial electronics are mostly finished goods, one can combine them to meet the basic cell–frequency requirement for the contingency table. Since the $\chi^2$ value is 22.240, which also exceeds the critical value at the one per cent significance level (13.81), the null hypothesis is rejected.

Table 7.7. **Contingency Table for Analysing the Relationship between Products and Types of Entry Mode**

| | Marketing subsidiaries | Production subsidiaries | Research subsidiaries | Total |
|---|---|---|---|---|
| Finished goods | 106 | 94 | 11 | 211 |
| Intermediate goods | 36 | 94 | 13 | 143 |
| **Total** | **142** | **188** | **24** | **354** |

$\chi^2$=22.240, contingency coefficient (cc) = 0.244, d.f. = 2

In addition to the differences in the establishment of entry modes across markets and products, Table 7.8 reveals differences in entry modes across firm sizes. All groups classified by firm size established more production than marketing subsidiaries and more marketing than R&D subsidiaries. The shares of the three modes vary across the groups, however. The share of production subsidiaries for SMEs is larger than that for LEs and for conglomerates, but LEs and conglomerates have relatively more marketing and R&D subsidiaries than SMEs. In fact, SMEs have no R&D subsidiaries at all.

Table 7.8. **Distribution of Entry Modes by Firm Size**

| | Marketing subsidiaries | Production subsidiaries | Research subsidiaries | Total |
|---|---|---|---|---|
| Conglomerates | 96 (41.5) | 112 (48.5) | 23 (10.0) | 231 (100) |
| LEs | 17 (43.6) | 21 (53.8) | 1 (2.6) | 39 (100) |
| SMEs | 29 (34.5) | 55 (65.5) | 0 (0.0) | 84 (100) |
| **Total** | **142 (40.1)** | **188 (53.1)** | **24 (6.8)** | **354 (100)** |

*Note:*   Figures in parentheses represent the percentage share of each type of subsidiary.

Table 7.9 tests the statistical significance of these differences, with LEs and conglomerates combined to meet the cell–frequency requirement. The null hypothesis is that there is no difference in the composition of entry modes across firm sizes. The $\chi^2$ is a little smaller than the critical value at the one per cent level (13.81), but larger than the critical value at the 5 per cent level (5.99). Thus, differences in entry modes across firms are not so prevalent as the differences across markets and products, but there probably exist significant differences in entry modes across firm sizes.

Table 7.9. **Contingency Table for Analysing the Relationship between Firm Size and Type of Entry Mode**

| | Marketing subsidiaries | Production subsidiaries | Research subsidiaries | Total |
|---|---|---|---|---|
| Conglomerates & LEs | 113 | 133 | 24 | 270 |
| SMEs | 29 | 55 | 0 | 84 |
| **Total (55)** | **142** | **188** | **24** | **354** |

$\chi^2$ =11.497, contingency coefficient (cc) = 0.177, d.f. = 2

## Differences in the Establishment of Production Subsidiaries

Table 7.10 shows that subsidiaries manufacturing parts and components are inclined to locate in developing countries. In contrast, consumer and industrial electronics production facilities tend to locate in both developed and developing countries.

Table 7.10. **Regional Distribution of Production Subsidiaries by Sector**

|  | Consumer electronics | Components & parts | Industrial electronics | Total |
|---|---|---|---|---|
| ASEAN | 14 | 26 | 5 | 45 |
| South Asia | 5 | 2 | 1 | 8 |
| China | 21 | 38 | 7 | 66 |
| NAFTA | 9 | 12 | 2 | 23 |
| EU | 14 | 11 | 3 | 28 |
| Others | 8 | 5 | 5 | 18 |
| **Total** | **71** | **94** | **23** | **188** |

Table 7.11 tests the statistical significance of this difference for subsidiaries manufacturing finished and intermediate goods, with consumer and industrial electronics combined. Statistically meaningful differences between finished and intermediate products could reveal whether product–specific reasons exist for the location of production subsidiaries — reasons that might arise from differences in the need for market proximity across products. Market proximity may be more crucial than factor cost for finished goods while factor cost may take precedence for intermediate goods. The null hypothesis is that there exist no differences in the regional distribution of production subsidiaries between finished and intermediate goods. The $\chi^2$ is smaller than the critical value at the 5 per cent level (7.81), so the null hypothesis is not rejected. Firms apparently do not consider product–specific factors in distributing manufacturing subsidiaries across regions. This result may stem from a problem associated with categorisation, however. As already noted, conglomerates, for example, can have different motives from those of other firms in distributing production subsidiaries for manufacturing intermediate goods. If so, the categories need more disaggregation.

Table 7.11. **Production Subsidiaries for Manufacturing Finished and Intermediate Goods**

|  | Finished goods | Intermediate goods | Total |
|---|---|---|---|
| **Developing Countries** |  |  |  |
| ASEAN & S. Asia | 25 (32.9) | 28 (31.5) | 53 (32.1) |
| China | 28 (34.1) | 38 (41.5) | 66 (38.0) |
| **Developed Counties** |  |  |  |
| NAFTA | 11 (13.5) | 12 (13.5) | 23 (13.5) |
| EU | 17 (19.5) | 11 (13.5) | 28 (16.4) |
| **Total** | **81 (100)** | **89 (100)** | **170 (100)** |

*Note:*  ASEAN & S. Asia are merged to meet the cell–frequency requirement. Figures in parentheses represent the percentage share of each type of subsidiary.
$\chi^2 = 2.644$, contingency coefficient (cc) = 0.124, d.f. = 3

Table 7.12 looks at differences between conglomerates and SMEs in distributing assembly and parts production functions abroad. For the four biggest conglomerates, the ratio of production subsidiaries for intermediate goods (parts) to those for finished goods is much larger in developed than in developing countries. This pattern reverses for "other firms", mostly SMEs. As already discussed, the four conglomerates have located subsidiaries to supply parts to established assembly subsidiaries for consumer electronics including CTVs, VCRs and micro–wave ovens (MWOs). They consider proximity to customers or suppliers as more important than factor–cost differentials. On the other hand, SMEs are mostly non–assemblers, and thus more interested in exploiting low factor costs in host countries. This contrasting pattern can support the argument that trade policy and production technology applicable in host countries affects the distribution of the value chain abroad. Businessmen from the big conglomerates, interviewed by the author, also confirm that they have established parts–manufacturing subsidiaries more in developed than in developing countries because developed countries generally impose stricter local–content rules.

Table 7.12. **The Ratio of Intermediate Goods to Finished Goods Manufacturing Subsidiaries**

| | Conglomerates | | | Other firms | | |
|---|---|---|---|---|---|---|
| | Finished goods(A) | Intermediate goods(B) | B/A | Finished goods(a) | Intermediate goods(b) | b/a |
| **Developing Countries** | | | | | | |
| ASEAN | 15 | 9 | 0.6 | 4 | 17 | 4.3 |
| South Asia | 5 | 1 | 0.2 | 1 | 1 | 1 |
| China | 21 | 11 | 0.52 | 7 | 27 | 3.8 |
| **Developed Countries** | | | | | | |
| NAFTA | 6 | 8 | 1.33 | 5 | 4 | 0.8 |
| EU | 11 | 8 | 0.73 | 6 | 3 | 0.5 |

$\chi^2 = \Sigma\{(O_i - E_i)^2/E_i\} = \Sigma\{(B/A - b/a)^2/b/a\} = 7.1118 > 5.99.$ ($\alpha$: 5 %, d.f. = 2)

The statistical significance test (in this case, a "goodness of fit" test) confirms this result. Suppose that b/a is the expected ratio and B/A the observed ratio. The null hypothesis is that the expected and observed ratios fit closely. The $\chi^2$ value (7.1118) exceeds the critical value (5.99) at the 5 per cent level, and the null hypothesis is rejected.

### *Different Processes of Globalisation: Three Big Electronics Conglomerates*

This section explores variations in the *order* of establishing subsidiaries across major markets, to obtain more dynamic evidence on the distribution of the value chain. Because the initial entry mode is critical in determining the development path of FDI, the first observations cover differences in initial entry modes across major markets. Table 7.13 shows that the initial entry modes of the three biggest Korean electronic firms differ greatly across major markets. Samsung, Daewoo and LG all established marketing subsidiaries at first in the EU and NAFTA, but started with assembly subsidiaries in ASEAN. They entered China with component–manufacturing subsidiaries.

The differences in initial entry modes inevitably determine different development paths of FDI across markets. In the EU and NAFTA, the natural progression of Korean FDI in consumer electronics has moved from marketing to assembly and then to parts production. Firms have shifted entry modes from marketing to assembly subsidiaries since the mid–1980s in order to avoid contingency protection. Because the shifts were forced, regardless of the availability of proper production technology suitable for those locations, some of their subsidiaries achieved poor performances, at least initially.

The viability of foreign subsidiaries often depends on intermediate inputs imported from the home country, but strict local–content rules did not allow them to maintain such a strategy. As a result, firms faced a decision constraint: to shift to higher modes or revert to marketing. Most subsidiaries established to circumvent restrictive trade policies have successfully adapted to the local markets and developed further to higher modes, but some reverted to initial entry modes. For instance, Samsung's assembly subsidiary established in Portugal in 1982 reverted to marketing in 1991. LG's assembly subsidiaries established in the United States in 1981 and in Germany in 1987 reverted to marketing in 1991 and 1995 respectively.

Table 7.13. **The Order of Establishing Foreign Subsidiaries**

|  |  | Marketing | Assembly | Common parts | Core parts | R&D | Regional headquarters |
|---|---|---|---|---|---|---|---|
| **EU** | Samsung | ①1982 | ②1987 | ③1990 | ④1990 | ⑤1996 | ⑥1994 |
|  | Daewoo | ①1988 | ②1988 | ③1993 | ④1993 | ⑤1993 | – |
|  | LG | ①1980 | ②1988 | ③1990 | ⑤1996 | ④1991 | – |
| **NAFTA** | Samsung | ①1978 | ②1988 | ③1994 | ④1994 | ⑤1994 | ⑥1996 |
|  | Daewoo | ①1976 | ②1990 | ③1995 | ④1997 | ⑤1997 | – |
|  | LG | ①1977 | ②1988 | ④1995 | – | ③1991 | – |
| **ASEAN** | Samsung | ④1995 | ①1988 | ②1990 | ③1990 | – | ⑤1995 |
|  | Daewoo LG | ③1997 | ①1990 | – | ②1993 | – | – |
|  |  | ②1988 | ①1988 | – | ③1993 | – | – |
| **China** | Samsung | – | ③1993 | ①1992 | ②1993 | ④1996 | ⑤1996 |
|  | Daewoo | – | – | ①1995 | ②1995 | – | – |
|  | LG | ④1995 | ③1995 | ①1994 | – | ②1994 | – |

*Source:*   Company data.

These markets have maintained different trade policies. The EU and NAFTA tend to use contingent protection, while most developing countries rely on effective standard protection. The varied entry modes reflect these differences. Korean consumer electronics firms could initially penetrate the EU and NAFTA through exports, because standard protection is relatively low there. In contrast, they experienced difficulties in penetrating some developing countries through exports because of relatively high standard protection. Chapter 3 claimed that firms shift particular segments of their value chains in response to specific trade policy instruments imposed by host countries. This evidence supports that claim.

In ASEAN, on the other hand, Korean FDI in consumer electronics has developed from assembly to parts manufacturing and then to marketing. Parts–manufacturing subsidiaries preceded marketing subsidiaries. The ASEAN countries maintain relatively high standard protection not only for finished but also for intermediate goods. Such circumstances make foreign production more favourable than exporting. In China, Korean consumer electronics firms invested first in common components, then expanded into core parts, developing assembly affiliates after that and marketing subsidiaries still later. Some of their investment in common components may have reflected delocalisation to exploit low labour costs, while effective trade protection in China might have attracted additional investment, including core–parts manufacturing and assembly. These findings generally coincide with the hypothetical path described in Figure 5.2.

Table 7.14 supports the hypothesis that, overall, firms deploy abroad more downstream activities than midstream or upstream ones. Although some sub–totals for individual firms do not exactly coincide with the hypothesis, the overall pattern is well in line with the arguments in Part One. Marketing subsidiaries account for the largest share in the total, followed by assembly, core production, common components, R&D and regional headquarters. Significant differences in the distribution of the value chain across regions do exist, however. In the EU and NAFTA, all three big firms deploy more marketing subsidiaries than assembly or parts–production subsidiaries, but they have more assembly subsidiaries than marketing subsidiaries in ASEAN. In China, they establish more parts–manufacturing subsidiaries than assembly or marketing subsidiaries.

Table 7.14. **Number of Foreign Subsidiaries Performing Different Functions in Major Target Markets**

| | | Marketing | Assembly | Common components | Core parts | R&D | Regional headquarters |
|---|---|---|---|---|---|---|---|
| EU | Samsung | 6 | 4 | 1 | 2 | 1 | 1 |
| | Daewoo | 5 | 3 | 2 | 2 | 1 | 0 |
| | LG | 6 | 1 | 1 | 1 | 1 | 0 |
| (Sub–total) | | 17 | 8 | 4 | 5 | 3 | 1 |
| NAFTA | Samsung | 3 | 1 | 1 | 1 | 1 | 1 |
| | Daewoo | 3 | 1 | 1 | 1 | 1 | 0 |
| | LG | 3 | 1 | 1 | 1 | 1 | 0 |
| (Sub–total) | | 9 | 3 | 3 | 3 | 3 | 1 |
| ASEAN | Samsung | 2 | 4 | 1 | 2 | 0 | 1 |
| | Daewoo | 1 | 3 | 0 | 1 | 0 | 0 |
| | LG | 1 | 5 | 0 | 1 | 0 | 0 |
| (Sub–total) | | 4 | 12 | 1 | 4 | 0 | 1 |
| China | Samsung | 0 | 3 | 2 | 3 | 0 | 1 |
| | Daewoo | 0 | 1 | 1 | 1 | 0 | 0 |
| | LG | 1 | 3 | 2 | 1 | 0 | 0 |
| (Sub–total) | | 1 | 7 | 5 | 5 | 0 | 1 |
| **Total** | | **31** | **30** | **13** | **17** | **6** | **4** |

Table 7.15 compares the rank order of the numbers of subsidiaries in Table 7.14 and the sequencing order of subsidiary establishment in Table 7.13. Among the 23 cases, 12 are slightly mismatched, including two of six in the EU and NAFTA and around half in ASEAN and China. Spearman's formula for rank correlation can reveal any statistical significance in the relationship between the order of establishing subsidiaries and the share of each mode in the total numbers of subsidiaries. The test rejects the null hypothesis of no relation between the two rankings. The value of Spearman's $\rho$ exceeds the critical value at the 5 per cent level for all major markets, and at the one per cent level for the EU and NAFTA. The number of foreign subsidiaries in each mode and their sequence order of establishment by mode are positively related.

Table 7.15. **Rank Correlation between Numbers of Subsidiaries and their Sequence Order of Establishment, by Mode**

| | EU | | NAFTA | | ASEAN | | China | |
|---|---|---|---|---|---|---|---|---|
| | I | II | I | II | I | II | I | II |
| Marketing | 1 | 1 | 1 | 1 | 3 | 4 | 4 | 5 |
| Assembly | 2 | 2 | 2 | 2 | 1 | 1 | 1 | 3 |
| Common components | 4 | 3 | 4 | 3 | 4 | 2 | 2 | 1 |
| Core parts | 3 | 4 | 3 | 4 | 2 | 3 | 3 | 2 |
| R&D | 5 | 5 | 5 | 5 | – | – | 5 | 4 |
| Regional headquarters | 6 | 6 | 6 | 6 | 5 | 5 | 6 | 6 |
| The Value of Spearman's $\rho$ | | | | | | | | |
| EU | | 0.94286 | | | ASEAN | | | 0.70000 |
| NAFTA | | 0.94286 | | | China | | | 0.77143 |

*Note:* In the upper part of the table, column I ranks the numbers of subsidiaries by mode; column II denotes the sequential order of their establishment by mode.

The findings in this chapter support several hypotheses made in Part One. Evidence of differences in the establishment of entry modes across firms, markets and products shows how factors specific to each affect the regional distribution of a firm's subsidiaries. Differences in the regional distribution of production subsidiaries between conglomerates and SMEs show indirectly that restrictive trade policies of host countries can affect their establishment. Differences in production volume across different locations can also serve as grounds for arguing that firms apply different production technologies in different countries. Differences in the order of establishing foreign subsidiaries give more direct evidence that market–specific factors can be critical in determining the distribution of a firm's value chain.

# Note

1. The method of empirical analyses in this part draws heavily from Jun (1985).

# Chapter 8

# The Determinants of FDI for the Globalisation of Corporate Activities

## A Conceptual Model

The findings in the previous chapter cannot directly identify the factors determining entry modes. An econometric analysis can accomplish that. Numerous studies have already applied various econometric models to identify the most significant variables associated with FDI. Some of them have noted cross–sectional differences in FDI or foreign production across firms, industries and locations. They use the rationale that factors specific to firms, industries and locations affect decisions to undertake FDI. Because some firms and some industries are more active in FDI than others, and some locations attract more FDI than others, studies have tried to identify the specific factors involved (see, for example, Swedenborg, 1979). Although there can be some variations in the composition and definition of variables, which often produce discrepancies in the estimates, Equation *(8.1)* below represents the basic structure of these earlier empirical efforts (for details, see United Nations, 1992). It simply states that FDI is a function of factors specific to firms, industries and locations.

$$FDI_{ijk} = f\left(\{F_i\},\, \{L_j\},\, \{I_k\}\right) \qquad\qquad (8.1)$$

where $FDI_{ijk}$ symbolises the amount of FDI by firm $i$ for its product $k$ in market $j$ while $\{F_i\}$ denotes a set of firm–specific factors of investing firm $i$; $\{L_j\}$ represents a set of location–specific factors of host country $j$; and $\{I_k\}$ symbolises a set of industry–specific factors of investing industry $k$.

Figure 6.1 (p. 67), however, suggests modification of this equation. First, one can use the different subsidiary modes rather than FDI itself as the dependent variable, because the choice of entry modes can reflect dynamic phenomena in FDI patterns. Next, one can replace the industry–specific and location–specific factors in Equation *(8.1)* with product–specific and market–specific factors, to seek evidence at a more microeconomic level.

Equation *(8.2)* posits functional relationships between modes of subsidiaries and three sets of exogenous variables, namely factors specific to firms, markets and products. This is not a new econometric model, but rather an extension of existing ones. With it, one can identify the main variables affecting entry–mode decisions. This can provide some clues regarding the dynamics of FDI.

$$MS_{ijk} = f(\{F_i\}, \{M_j\}, \{P_k\}) \tag{8.2}$$

where $MS_{ijk}$ symbolises mode of subsidiary of firm $i$ for its product $k$ in market $j$ while $\{M_j\}$ $j$ and $\{P_k\}$ represent a set of market–specific factors of market $j$ and a set of product–specific factors of product $k$.

The investigation faces two major challenges — how to categorise different modes of subsidiaries and how to select the exogenous variables. The first problem derives mainly from difficulties in categorising subsidiaries by mode. Foreign subsidiaries are not necessarily distinguishable because most of them were established or developed to conduct a cluster of functions. The second problem arises from difficulties in both selection and measurement.

**Operational Definition of Variables and Their Functional Relationship**

Chapter 6 presented a dynamic framework for investment decision making. This framework suggests a guideline for selecting or organising the variables to capture dynamic changes in entry modes. Previous chapters also contended that trade policies of host countries and production technologies of investing firms affect the distribution of the value chain. The variables selected are relevant to investigating the validity of all these arguments. They do not exhaust the list of potentially important determinants of FDI, but do include the main items that seem to be relevant to the framework in Figure 6.1. The list of variables is as follows:

*Endogenous variables*

$MS_{ijk}$ = 1 for marketing subsidiary,

2 for production subsidiary,

3 for R&D subsidiary, and

4 for regional headquarters.

### Exogenous variables

#### (1) Firm–Specific Factors

i) *R&D* = average ratio of the parent firm's total R&D expenditure to its sales in three recent years (1994–96).

ii) *ECO* = a simple rank value of the size of business group at the end of 1996 (1: SMEs, 5: five largest conglomerates).

iii) *FMO* = the average proportion of exports to total sales of the parent firm in 1994–96.

#### (2) Market–Specific Factors

i) *WGD* = the sum of ratios of the average wage level of domestic operations to that of foreign operations by trisected equivalent employed groups at the end of 1996.

ii) *CPS* = questionnaire responses that compare subsidiary locations with the home country in terms of compatibility with flexible production systems, using a five–point scale (1: hardly compatible, 5: highly compatible).

iii) *MSZ* = the ratio of the current or expected target–market size (including host and other target markets) to the production level at which foreign affiliates could exploit scale economies at the end of 1996.

iv) *RTP* = questionnaire responses estimating the level of restrictions, again on a five–point scale (1: no restriction, 5: extremely restrictive).

#### (3) Product–Specific Factors

i) *RCA* = Balassa's index of revealed comparative advantage in 1994.

ii) *MPX* = questionnaire responses estimating the degree of a product's need for market proximity, on another five–point scale (1: fairly low, 5: fairly high).

The paragraphs below provide the operational definitions of the variables, as crafted to measure each variable more logically given the limited availability of data. The functional relationship between dependent and independent variables is dealt with in the discussion of each variable. One can expect that the sign and value of its coefficient in the regression will indicate the influence of each exogenous variable on the endogenous variable.

## Dependent Variables

Chapter 6 maintained that foreign subsidiaries can be classified into several functional modes: marketing, final assembly, sub–assembly and components manufacturing, core processing or key–parts manufacturing, R&D and regional headquarters. Data on some foreign subsidiaries are detailed enough to allow such distinctions (see Tables 7.13 and 7.14). Not all subsidiaries bear classification at these levels, however, because the directory published by the EIAK does not provide sufficiently detailed information. Under this constraint, the analysis uses the rather simple EIAK classification, namely marketing subsidiaries, production subsidiaries, R&D subsidiaries and regional headquarters. To make the model operational, it assigns a numerical value to each mode, as described in the listing above.

## Independent Variables

As specified in Equation (8.2), independent variables include variables specific to firms, products and markets. The composition of variables and their measurement can vary, depending on the purposes of a study, and the variables selected and defined operationally here are specific variables relevant to the previous discussion. The operational definitions specify how the variables are measured, along with a review of the arguments for possible causality and the expected influence of each independent variable on FDI. This establishes the rationale for inclusion of each variable.

### Firm–Specific Factors

Firms' characteristics are proxies for internal resources, which can be distinguished as advantages related to a specific production technology and advantages of organisation and management in general. The accumulation of R&D capability would relate closely to the technological advantages. Because it is often impossible to measure, most studies have used investment in R&D as a surrogate variable. Organisational advantages, on the other hand, grow with experience and can develop through the accumulation of management techniques (Andersson and Arvidsson, 1993). The age or size of a parent firm could serve as a proxy for these advantages but, because some parent firms belong to larger business groups, data on a single parent company can be inappropriate. This study therefore uses economic concentration, a more comprehensive measurement of these advantages. Moreover, and aside from organisational factors, management attitudes also can affect investment decision making, as discussed in Chapter 6. Other things equal, for example, firms with risk–taking management will invest abroad more than will those with risk–averse management. This analysis employs an export–orientation measure as a surrogate for such management attitudes.

*R&D Intensity (R&D).* Firms' technological advantages constitute one of the most important factors determining foreign investment. Established FDI theory notes how they can exploit these advantages through foreign production. Because firms can accumulate them through *R&D* activities, *R&D* intensity has a positive relationship to the overall propensity to produce abroad. Many economists, including Swedenborg (1979), found empirical evidence supporting this conjecture. For the same reason, one expects a firm's *R&D* intensity to have a positive causal relationship with the propensity to establish higher subsidiary entry modes. Yet its significance may vary with types of FDI, being more important, for example, for offensive horizontal expansion than for delocalisation.

*R&D* intensity can be measured as the ratio of the firm's current *R&D* expenditures to its sales, as is done here. The logical variable would be the outstanding amount of intangible assets accumulated through *R&D* activities, but data constraints do not allow this measurement. Although the cost of inputs and the value of outputs cannot necessarily substitute for each other, over a long period a positive relationship between the two can be established. *R&D* effort must serve as a proxy for *R&D* results. Because *R&D* results are freely mobile within an international firm, it would be theoretically more correct to use a firm's total *R&D* expenditures, regardless of whether *R&D* activities are located at home or abroad. Likewise, total sales would make a better denominator for the measure. The available data, however, permit only the use of the ratio calculated from the parent firm's *R&D* expenditures and sales. The operational definition is the average ratio of *R&D* expenditures to sales in 1994–96.

*Economic Concentration (ECO).* Firms maintaining dominant positions in their industries in the home country can establish their subsidiaries in foreign markets more easily. They are in fact inclined to expand foreign operation to avoid domestic regulations on oligopolistic firms. One therefore can expect a positive correlation between the economic concentration level of a firm and its propensity to undertake investment abroad. Pugel (1981) found a significant positive relationship between the concentration ratio and FDI in his study of investments of US industries. Pearce (1989) found a similar result. Owen (1982), on the other hand, found no significant relationship between FDI and the Herfindahl index[1].

Korean industry has a unique pattern of economic concentration, characterised not only by conglomerates' dominant positions in some major industries but also by their diversification into various industries. In fact, more diversified firms often can absorb the risk of international operation more easily and have better access to financial and human resources for foreign operations. Hence, the leading Korean conglomerates, which are highly dominant and diversified in many industries, are in a better position to invest abroad than other firms.

This unique characteristic, however, cannot be measured by an index either for concentration or for diversification[2]. Therefore, this study needs a different measure. Korea's Fair Trade Commission has announced lists of products under oligopolistic competition, and of large business groups that the commission regulates separately. Based on these lists, the measure used assigns values of one for small and medium–size companies, two for large companies with sales between $100 million and $1 billion, three for large companies with sales of over $1 billion, four for the 30 largest business groups and five for the five largest groups at the end of 1996. This variable should have a positive relation to entry–mode levels.

*Foreign–Market Orientation (FMO)*. The managements of exporting firms have a relatively high propensity for risk–taking compared with those of non–exporting firms. This tendency also applies to foreign investment. Firms oriented towards foreign markets are more likely to invest in target markets than those oriented towards domestic markets. Piercy (1981) found a high correlation between export ratios and the contributions of foreign sales to total sales. This could serve as grounds for arguing that FDI has a positive impact on home–country exports, but the relationship between exports and FDI is too complicated to be addressed in this very generalised way. This issue receives separate discussion in Chapter 9. The focus here is on how much this variable can serve as a firm–specific factor explaining a decision to invest abroad. Its operational measure is the average proportion of export to total sales of a parent firm in 1994–96. A positive relationship should obtain between this measure and entry–mode levels, which implies simply that exporting firms would be more active in investment abroad than non–exporting firms.

### Market–Specific Factors

A firm's locational decision can depend on various factors, as studies on locational determinants of FDI illustrate[3]. This analysis selects variables representing not only production–cost differentials between home and host countries, but also market opportunities and security considerations of investing firms, following the framework presented earlier. The comparison of labour costs and the degrees of industrialisation between host and home countries can proxy for production–cost differentials. Market size and market growth rates can represent market opportunities, while trade policies of host countries, such as local–content requirements, restrictions on imports and regional trading blocs can be proxies for market security.

*Wage differentials (WGD)*. Despite its decreasing weight in total production cost, labour cost remains an important factor determining the location of FDI. Firms distribute their value chains from high to low labour–cost sites to take advantage of wage differentials. Because labour–cost differentials do not capture the quality of human capital, they alone cannot proxy for the marginal productivity of labour. Some studies use unit labour cost differentials as a measure of this variable (Adams, 1992). Culem (1988), for instance, found that unit labour–cost differentials between host and home countries have a significant negative impact on FDI. The total wage cost per worker of a firm in its domestic relative to its foreign operations can also be a possible surrogate for wage differentials (Swedenborg, 1979). Measuring it is also problematic, however, because wage employees are not homogeneous. Most employees in assembly subsidiaries, for example, would be factory workers, while those in *R&D* subsidiaries must be scientists or researchers.

This study surveys the wage levels of foreign operations relative to domestic ones by trisected equivalent employee groups to take into account the different compositions of employees across various modes of subsidiaries. The operational measure is the sum of the respective ratios, where the denominators are the average wage levels of foreign affiliates and the numerators are the average wage levels of parent firms at the end of 1996 — both measured for equivalent trisected employee groups. Data on the related average wage levels were obtained from a questionnaire completed by company experts. Because lower labour–cost locations are awarded higher values, this variable should have a positive relationship with offensive horizontal integration and delocalisation. It should not greatly influence FDI for vertical integration and defensive horizontal integration, however.

*Compatibility with Flexible Production Systems (CPS).* As Chapter 4 pointed out, firms can significantly reduce labour costs for unskilled workers — and their weight in total production costs — while depending more on skilled workers through the adoption of new, flexible production systems. In this process, the availability of skilled workers, the development of telecommunication and other industrial infrastructures and the existence of related industrial clusters, including parts suppliers, become critical. This suggests that the new systems may alter the cost structures of firms and the elements of locational advantage.

Flexible production systems are applicable only in countries with well–developed industrial infrastructures and related industries. Indices for infrastructure quality and the degree of industrialisation thus might serve as proxies for a CPS variable. A Business International (BI) data set includes country scores on perceived desirability from the perspective of these factors[4], and Wheeler and Mody (1992) found positive relationships between FDI from the United States and these indices. Nevertheless, these measures do not necessarily coincide with locational compatibility with flexible production systems, as perceived by Korean firms, because various other factors affect it. For this reason, this study once again uses direct survey results from a simple questionnaire to construct data for this variable. The operational measure captures answers to a question asking respondents to rank compatibility on a five–point scale, from lowest (one) to highest (five). The question was, "Considering the proximity of parts suppliers, skilled workers and infrastructure, how did you evaluate the location, when you made a decision to invest there, in terms of compatibility with a flexible production system in comparison with the home country?" While it is difficult to have an *a priori* notion of the sign on the coefficient for this variable in regressions with entry–mode levels in particular countries, one can expect a positive relationship with some types of investments, including offensive horizontal expansion in developed countries.

*Market Size (MSZ)*. Many empirical studies, for instance Swedenborg (1979) and Kobrin (1976), use GNP or GDP to measure the market size and find them positively related to FDI outflows. In general, the larger the aggregate size of the foreign market, the larger the demand for goods. Other studies use per capita GDP. Root and Ahmed (1979), and Schneider and Frey (1985) found that per capita GDP has a positive influence. The growth rate of the host country is often cited as another factor attracting FDI. Root and Ahmed (1979) found this for developing countries.

Jun (1985) suggests a much more specific measure, namely the dollar value of consumption of a given product in each host country. Consumption volume, however, does not reflect product–specific attributes like different economic scales of production, and studies using it have not noted that most FDI projects aim for exports to third countries, especially neighbouring markets in trading blocs. The variable used here is the ratio of target–market size to the production levels at which affiliates can exploit scale economies in host countries (end–1996 data). Target–market size represents estimated consumption volume in both host countries and other major markets to which affiliates currently export or intend to export. The data on firm–specific and product–specific market size were, once again, supplied by companies in a survey questionnaire. This variable is expected to have a positive relationship with most forms of horizontal expansion.

*Restrictive Trade Policy (RTP)*. Each restrictive trade policy can have a separate variable in empirical tests, because measurement of individual policies should differ greatly. Many studies do estimate the relationship between individual trade policies and FDI flows or stocks. Saunders (1982), for instance, used tariff rates to find a relationship between protection and FDI inflows. Barrell and Pain (1993) chose the cumulated stock of antidumping (AD) cases for a similar test. Wheeler and Mody (1992) use indices of local–content requirements constructed by Business International, Inc. Swedenborg (1979) applies a dummy variable for trading blocs.

In contrast, an integrated variable can proxy for the effective protection of a given industry. The effective rate of protection (ERP) is a good surrogate because conceptually it measures protection more comprehensively. Heitger and Stehn (1990) use a constructed ERP index to find a positive relationship with Japanese investment in the EC[5]. The ERP concept tries to assess the effect of output protection on the size of an economic activity when inputs used in the production of that output are also protected. Yet it measures only effects on value added per unit of output and avoids the important issue of how much output itself would change in response to the protection. Moreover, this study has insisted that individual trade policies have different influences on the spatial distribution of the value chain, and firms distribute their value chains abroad not only to respond to actual enforcement of trade barriers but also to prepare for possible actions in the future.

The study thus needs an integrated measure representing levels of protection that host countries actually applied or were expected to apply. In the survey questionnaire, parents and affiliates experts were asked, "How did you estimate the level of restrictive trade policy actually applied or expected to be applied by host countries when you made a decision to invest there?" Responses were qualitative, ranging along a five–point scale (one = no restriction; five = extremely restrictive trade policy). This variable should correlate strongly with investment, especially for defensive horizontal expansion.

### Product–Specific Factors

Although numerous variables can represent product–specific factors affecting firms' decisions to invest abroad, the main task here is to find whether such factors have an effect on a firm's choice of entry mode. The focus lies on two variables relevant to the discussion — export competitiveness, proxied by an index of revealed comparative advantage (RCA), and the need for market proximity.

*Competitiveness of Product (RCA).* An *RCA* index compares the share that a given item holds in a country's total exports with the share of that item in world exports[6]. It does not show either the volume of trade or the country's share of a given export market. It has a tendency to be high with export concentration in the item and low with export diversification. With these limitations, the index and changes in it sometimes cannot explain how much competitiveness a country has in a certain item. Some other index must often support its use.

Many studies use the *RCA* index as a proxy for product competitiveness because it is convenient and alternatives are difficult to obtain. Most of those studies find positive relationships between the *RCA* and FDI outflows. Heitger and Stehn (1990), for instance, use *RCA* as a proxy for firm–specific intangible assets and find positive evidence. Lee and Plummer (1992) also find that outward FDI will more likely flow from sectors that show high *RCA*s in world export markets, regardless of whether they are decreasing or increasing. They further identify FDI from an industry with a high but declining *RCA* as defensive and FDI from an industry with a high and increasing *RCA* as aggressive. Kojima (1982), on the other hand, contends that FDI by an industry whose *RCA* is declining is trade–oriented, whereas other cases involve anti–trade FDI.

This study also uses an *RCA* index as a surrogate for the product competitiveness of Korean electronics firms that invest abroad, calculated on the base of Korean industry's trade with the rest of the world in 1994. It should have a positive relationship with some types of investments, including offensive horizontal expansion in developed countries, but its trend may associate differently with different types of FDI. For example, delocalisation can appear when *RCA* is not low but declining whereas horizontal expansion in developed markets occurs when *RCA* is not high but increasing.

*Need for Market Proximity (MPX).* Advertising intensity can proxy for the need for market proximity because advertising–intensive products require a local presence. Many studies find empirical evidence that advertising expenditure as a percentage of sales can be a positive determinant of FDI. Saunders (1982) and Kumar (1987) found this for Canada and India, respectively. Market–service variables can also serve. Kirkpatrick and Yamin (1981) found after–sales services as a percentage of sales to be a significant determinant of FDI. Lee (1986) discovered similar evidence using the frequency of pre–sales and after–sales services.

This analysis needs a more comprehensive measure to find variations in the determinants across different types of FDI and subsidiaries. To develop it, the questionnaire asked respondents, "How did you estimate the need for market proximity for the product or industry in which you invested abroad?" The operational measure emerged once again from responses on a five–point scale, with higher needs for market proximity awarded higher values.

Part One argued that firms' downstream activities need higher market proximity than upstream activities, based on the facts of firms' tendency to establish more downstream subsidiaries than upstream ones. One thus expects that this measure has a positive relationship with the propensity to establish downstream subsidiaries abroad, although it reflects product–specific factors. There can be variations across different types of FDI. Market proximity may be a more significant determinant for horizontal investment than for vertical investment or delocalisation.

## Model Specification and Methodology

The correlation matrix of the explanatory variables shows that some of them are correlated with each other. For instance, *WGD* is highly correlated with *CPS*. In addition, *ECO, WGD* and *R&D* are fairly, if not closely, correlated with *MPX, MSZ* and *MPX*, respectively. To avoid the problem of multicollinearity in the specified model, corresponding variables should be omitted. Here, *CPS* is dropped but the remaining variables stay in the model because they relate primarily to the arguments in Part One. Thus eight variables remain for estimation, namely *ECO, R&D, FMO, WGD, MSZ, RTP, MPX,* and *RCA*. The model specification is as follows:

$$P[\,MS_n = l\,] = F_l(\alpha_0 + \alpha_1 ECO_n + \alpha_2 R\&D_n + \alpha_3 FMO_n + \alpha_4 WGD_n + \alpha_5 MSZ_n + \alpha_6 RTP_n$$
$$+ \alpha_7 MPX_n + \alpha_8 RCA_n), \quad l=1,2,3,4. \tag{8.3}$$

The model tests the hypothesised relationships by means of multiple regression analysis across firms, markets, and products. The categorical nature of the dependent variable limits application of the methodology, however. It is both qualitative and ordinal, because different modes reflect different levels of market commitment. Therefore, the model must accommodate its ordinal nature. The specific model is a multinomial ordered probit model that yields consistent parameter estimates applying a non–linear, maximum–likelihood estimation procedure[7]. It enables examination not only of the direction of relationships between a dependent variable and a set of independent variables but also of the statistical significance of each independent variable[8].

Table 8.1 summarises the descriptive statistics of each variable. It also presents their expected directions of influence on the dependent variable, which, except for *MPX*, should generally be positive; their measurements are designed that way. As we discussed in the previous section, however, discrepancies may exist depending on the type of FDI. To handle this, the sample will be classified in several ways, with separate coefficient estimations applying the probit model mentioned above, to examine variations in the determinants of the dependent variable across classified sub–samples.

Table 8.1. **Descriptive Statistics of the Sample**

| Variable | Mean | Standard Deviation | Expected sign |
|---|---|---|---|
| MS | 1.7119 | 0.6750 | |
| ECO | 4.0332 | 1.5235 | + |
| R&D | 7.3666 | 5.4436 | + |
| FMO | 0.6906 | 0.1801 | + |
| WGD | 3.3352 | 1.4205 | + |
| MPX | 3.1191 | 1.2604 | − |
| RTP | 1.1302 | 1.6080 | + |
| MSZ | 3.3186 | 1.1455 | + |
| RCA | 3.0378 | 2.1996 | + |

## Results of the Estimation

Table 8.2 presents the results of the regression analysis. As expected, they show that all variables except *ECO* and *MPX* correlate positively with the dependent variable — but all of the parameters are not necessarily statistically significant. *ECO, FMO,* and *RTP* are significant at the one per cent level, while *R&D* and *WGD* are significant at the 5 per cent level. The positive coefficients on *R&D, FMO, WGD* and *RTP* indicate that these variables are positively correlated to the propensity to establish higher entry modes. The negative coefficient for *ECO*, on the other hand, implies that firm size has an inverse relationship with the propensity to establish higher modes of subsidiaries, which does not coincide with earlier conjecture. The remaining variables play relatively minor roles, possibly because of differences in attributes across various types of FDI, which will be dealt with separately.

Overall, however, the results of the estimation are fairly satisfactory, as shown by the two different measures of explanatory power of the model. First, the chi–square value of the likelihood ratio test, which measures the explanatory power as a whole, was extremely favourable; one can reject at a highly significant level the null hypothesis that all parameters are equal to 0. Second, calculations of the percentage of correctly predicted cases also produced satisfactory results. One can confidently argue that the exogenous variables as a group can be a factor determining variations in the endogenous variable.

The statistical insignificance of explanatory variables like *MPX* and *RCA* might occur because Korean electronics firms engage in different types of FDI determined by different factors. To verify this, the sample may be grouped in several ways, not only to observe some otherwise statistically insignificant variables as significant in the sub–samples, but also to investigate variations in the determinants across different sub–samples. The first experiment separates the sample into two sub–samples: subsidiaries of conglomerates and of SMEs.

**Table 8.2. Results of Multinomial Cross–Sectional Estimation for the Sample of All Subsidiaries**

| Variables | Coefficients | t-statistic |
|---|---|---|
| Constant | -1.4752 | -2.412 |
| ECO | -0.2162 | -3.035 |
| R&D | 0.0364 | 2.179 |
| FMO | 1.4807 | 2.912 |
| WGD | 0.1331 | 2.238 |
| MPX | -0.0152 | -0.163 |
| RTP | 0.4410 | 5.074 |
| MSZ | 0.1296 | 1.486 |
| RCA | 0.0302 | 0.925 |
| Chi-square value of the likelihood ratio test | 123.8073 | |
| Percentage of correctly predicted cases | 73.13 | |
| Sample size | 361 | |

The results from applying the probit model appear in Table 8.3. In addition to *ECO, FMO* and *RTP*, *WGD* and *MSZ* exert strong influence, significant at the one per cent level, on the choice of entry mode in the sample for both SMEs and conglomerates. Moreover, they show a clear difference in determinants of entry modes between the two sub–samples. The impact of *RTP* on the conglomerates' propensity to establish higher entry modes is highly significant, whereas its impact on the SMEs' FDI decisions is insignificant. Similarly, *MSZ* plays an important role in the choice of entry modes by conglomerates, while it is not a crucial factor for SMEs. The parameter estimates for *WGD, MPX* and *R&D* show opposite signs for conglomerates and SMEs. For SMEs, the parameter coefficient for *WGD* is positive, which indicates that low labour costs exert a strong positive effect on SMEs' propensity to establish higher modes of subsidiaries. In contrast, conglomerates have a negative coefficient for *WGD*, which suggests a negative effect for them. Conglomerates have a negative parameter coefficient for *MPX*, while SMEs have a positive one. This indicates that conglomerates invest abroad more in downstream activities for products that require high market proximity, whereas SMEs have an opposite tendency. Similarly, the *R&D* parameter is positively signed for conglomerates and negatively signed for SMEs. This suggests that *R&D* has a positive impact on the conglomerates' propensity to establish higher modes and a negative impact for SMEs.

To observe additional variations in the determinants across different sub–samples, separate estimations were conducted for subsidiaries established in developed and developing countries. The results, summarised in Table 8.4, show the influence of most independent variables as different in significance or direction between the two sub–samples. *RTP* remains highly significant in the choice of entry mode in developed countries, but becomes less significant in developing countries. The *MSZ* variable behaves similarly between two sub–samples. This implies that firms tend to respond more sensitively to restrictive trade policies and market size in choosing entry modes in developed than in developing countries. Contrarily, the impact of *WGD* on the choice of entry modes is highly significant in developing countries but negligible in

92

Table 8.3. **Results of Multinomial Estimates for Two Sub–Samples: Subsidiaries of Conglomerates and of SMEs**

| Variables | Coefficients (t-statistics) | |
| --- | --- | --- |
| | Conglomerates | SMEs |
| Constant | –2.5764(–2.623) | –3.5955(–2.267) |
| R&D | 0.0393(1.739) | –0.0299(–0.647) |
| FMO | 1.6461(1.939) | 1.2274(1.108) |
| WGD | –0.0693(–0.990) | 0.6681(4.153) |
| MPX | –0.1645(–1.203) | 0.3684(1.357) |
| RTP | 0.5406(5.239) | 0.4114(1.606) |
| MSZ | 0.4362(3.403) | 0.0450(0.259) |
| RCA | –0.0265(–0.453) | 0.0220(0.315) |
| Chi–square value of the likelihood ratio test | 126.4736 | 59.2221 |
| Percentage of correctly predicted cases | 73.95 | 85.54 |
| Sample size | 238 | 123 |

*Note:*     ECO is excluded from the estimation because all conglomerates fall in same firm-size category. Figures in parenthesis following coefficient estimates are t-statistics.

developed countries. This may suggest that firms are sensitive to low labour costs when investing in developing countries, while they are not a major consideration for FDI to developed countries. The influence of *MPX* on the choice of entry modes also differs between the two sub–samples. Its coefficient is positively signed for affiliates in the developed countries, which indicates that firms have a propensity to establish higher entry modes there when *MPX* rises. In contrast, it is negatively signed for affiliates in developing countries, which implies a tendency to establish subsidiaries for downstream activities when *MPX* is increased. The coefficient is not statistically significant in either case, however.

These findings support the common notion that firms establish affiliates in developed countries to seek markets and in developing countries to save costs. Many empirical surveys have already found similar evidence. The most frequently cited motive to invest in developed countries is to circumvent trade barriers or exploit market potentials, but firms cite low labour costs as the primary motive to invest in developing countries.

This study confirms, for Korean electronics firms, the importance of *RTP* and *MSZ* in investment decisions in developed countries, and of *WGD* for investment in developing countries. If firms invest in developing countries to serve third markets, however, as often occurs, *RTP* and *MSZ* in host countries cannot be meaningful factors.

The estimated results may be biased by the overwhelming share of marketing and production subsidiaries and the negligible portion of *R&D* subsidiaries and regional headquarters in the sample. To address this problem, the four different modes reflected in the dependent variable have been combined into two groups, namely vertical and horizontal integration modes. The establishment of production subsidiaries represents horizontal integration, because most such subsidiaries conduct a cluster of functions, including manufacturing. The other modes are classed as vertical integration. The dependent variable takes values of zero for vertical integration and one for horizontal integration. This dichotomous structure suggests use of a binomial probit model.

Table 8.4. **Results of Multinomial Estimates for Two Separated Sub–samples of Subsidiaries in Developed and Developing Countries**

| Variables | Coefficients (t–statistics) | |
| --- | --- | --- |
| | Subsidiaries in DCs | Subsidiaries in LDCs. |
| Constant | −3.4540(−3.038) | −1.5605(−1.366) |
| ECO | −0.0516(−0.480) | −0.2216(−1.429) |
| R&D | 0.0414(1.410) | 0.0145(0.370) |
| FMO | 1.4184(1.731) | 1.1385(1.085) |
| WGD | 0.0991(0.677) | 0.4752(4.609) |
| MPX | 0.0827(0.588) | −0.2933(−1.346) |
| RTP | 0.6928(5.207) | 0.4713(2.884) |
| MSZ | 0.3228(1.912) | 0.1539(0.795) |
| RCA | −0.8531E−03(−0.016) | 0.0319(0.359) |
| Chi–square value of the likelihood ratio test | 95.0364 | 84.3116 |
| Percentage of correctly predicted cases | 77.65 | 90.58 |
| Sample size | 170 | 191 |

*Note:*    Figures in parenthesis following coefficient estimates are t-statistics.

Table 8.5 summarises the results. *RTP* and *WGD* are positively signed and statistically significant at the one per cent level, while *ECO* and *R&D* are negatively signed and statistically significant at the 5 per cent level. The positive coefficient on *WGD* indicates that the propensity to establish affiliates for horizontal integration relates positively to low labour costs in host countries. The positive coefficient for *RTP* suggests that strong trade barriers tend to stimulate the establishment of production subsidiaries, as the only way to gain access to highly protected markets. The negative coefficients for *ECO* and *R&D* imply that firms with large sales volumes and high R&D intensity tend to move more towards vertical integration than towards horizontal integration. These modifications in the model improve the overall estimation performance too. The chi–square value of the likelihood ratio test has substantially improved, from 123.8 to 239.8. The percentage of correctly predicted cases also improved to 85.50 per cent from 73.13 per cent.

Other applications of the binomial probit model reveal other differences in the determinants of globalisation across different groups. Table 8.6 shows the results for two sub–samples containing subsidiaries that manufacture finished goods and those that make intermediate products. The coefficients for *RPT* and *WGD* show positive signs in both cases, but the statistical significance of their influence differs substantially. That for *WGD* is higher for the intermediate–goods sub–sample than for finished goods. *RTP*, on the other hand, is highly significant for finished goods but less significant for intermediate products. The coefficient for *MPX* is negative for finished goods and positive for intermediate goods. These findings show that the most significant determinant of Korean firms' decisions in establishing production subsidiaries for manufacturing finished goods, mostly consumer electronics, is to circumvent restrictive trade measures. They also confirm low labour cost as the most significant factor in decisions to establish

Table 8.5. **Results of Binomial Cross–Sectional Estimation for the Sample of All Subsidiaries**

| Variables | Coefficients | t–statistics |
|---|---|---|
| *Constant* | −0.8035 | −1.111 |
| *ECO* | −0.1890 | −2.482 |
| *R&D* | −0.0418 | −2.069 |
| *FMO* | 0.4899 | 0.921 |
| *WGD* | 0.5214 | 5.890 |
| *MPX* | −0.1765 | −1.803 |
| *RTP* | 0.6351 | 7.723 |
| *MSZ* | −0.0837 | −0.774 |
| *RCA* | 0.0281 | 0.651 |
| Chi–square value of the likelihood ratio test | 239.7806 | |
| Percentage of correctly predicted cases | 85.50 | |
| Sample size | 361 | |

production subsidiaries for intermediate goods. They are consistent with the earlier findings that firms establish more production subsidiaries for intermediate goods in developing countries and more affiliates to make finished goods in developed countries.

It is not surprising that *MPX* is not significant in these estimations. It should exert strong influence on FDI for manufacturing finished goods, but not on FDI for intermediate goods. Physical proximity of production to markets has more importance for some products, but marketing is more critical for others. The specification used cannot verify these differences. This calls for new estimations, using two sub–samples composed of conglomerates and SMEs, and assuming that each group manufactures abroad products with different market–proximity characteristics. Table 8.7 shows the influence of *MPX* as significant for both conglomerates and SMEs, but in opposite directions. Its parameter estimate is negative for conglomerates but positive for SMEs. The net effect for the whole sample, naturally, becomes statistically insignificant. *RCA* has no significant influence on either sub–sample, which might be due to the deficiency of the measure. Many production affiliates make limited product ranges while most marketing affiliates sell more varied products. This inevitably distorts the measurement of this variable in terms of product classifications.

This chapter has found that the determinants of FDI differ across different sub–groups categorised by attributes of firms, host countries and products. Most notably, SMEs respond more sensitively to labour costs than do conglomerates, while conglomerates are more vulnerable to protective trade measures than SMEs. Restrictive trade measures strongly trigger FDI to developed countries, while cheap labour mainly motivates FDI to developing countries. Further, Korean firms establish production subsidiaries for finished goods, mostly consumer electronics, to circumvent restrictive trade measures, while they establish production subsidiaries for intermediate products to exploit low labour costs.

**Table 8.6. Results of Binomial Estimates for Two Sub–Samples of Affiliates Making Finished and Intermediate Goods**

| Variables | Coefficients (t–statistics) | |
| --- | --- | --- |
| | Finished goods | Intermediate goods |
| *Constant* | −0.4817(−0.489) | −1.5783(−1.303) |
| *ECO* | −0.2846(−2.155) | −0.0392(−0.338) |
| *R&D* | −0.0644(−2.247) | −0.0275(−0.733) |
| *FMO* | 0.2026(0.249) | 0.2870(0.312) |
| *WGD* | 0.4129(3.165) | 0.6850(5.054) |
| *MPX* | −0.0948(−0.671) | 0.1755(0.959) |
| *RTP* | 0.8015(7.214) | 0.1489(0.976) |
| *MSZ* | −0.0280(−0.177) | −0.1005(−0.609) |
| *RCA* | 0.0490(0.764) | −0.0970(−1.250) |
| Chi–square value of the likelihood ratio test | 163.5843 | 82.8619 |
| Percentage of correctly predicted cases | 86.18 | 85.42 |
| Sample size | 217 | 144 |

*Note:*    Figures in parenthesis following coefficient estimates are t–statistics.

**Table 8.7. Results of Binomial Estimation for Two Sub–Samples: Subsidiaries of Conglomerates and of SMEs**

| Variables | Coefficients (t–statistics) | |
| --- | --- | --- |
| | Conglomerates | SMEs |
| *Constant* | −1.3726(−1.154) | −3.5938(−2.542) |
| *R&D* | −0.0100(−0.387) | −0.0983(−2.171) |
| *FMO* | 1.2491(1.345) | 1.3076(1.526) |
| *WGD* | 0.4651(4.162) | 0.7887(4.776) |
| *MPX* | −0.4271(−3.119) | 0.4722(2.197) |
| *RTP* | 0.6519(7.555) | 0.8624(2.942) |
| *MSZ* | −0.1043(−0.646) | −0.0604(−0.353) |
| *RCA* | 0.0062(0.102) | −0.0382(−0.595) |
| Chi–square value of the likelihood ratio test | 174.5142 | 81.5923 |
| Percentage of correctly predicted cases | 88.24 | 86.18 |
| Sample size | 238 | 123 |

*Notes:*    ECO is excluded from the estimation, because all conglomerates fall in same firm–size category.
Figures in parenthesis following coefficient estimates are t–statistics.

Based on these findings, one can conclude that restrictive trade measures exert a highly significant impact on investments of conglomerates for finished goods in developed countries, while labour costs have a significant effect on investments of SMEs for intermediate goods in developing countries. These results are consistent with the earlier hypotheses that different types of FDI have different critical determinants. Although differences in the determinants across different types of FDI are not investigated, owing to difficulties associated with the distinction of different types of FDI, the statistical findings strongly support these hypotheses.

# Notes

1. The Herfindahl index can be measured as follows : $H = \{\sum_{1}^{n} Xi^2\} / \{\sum_{1}^{n} Xi\}^2$ ; $0 \leq H \leq 1$ where the $Xi$'s are the value of the firm's output in industries 1 through $n$.

2. To measure diversification, one can use the inverse Herfindahl index, Div = 1 – H. The index ranges from zero, when a firm produces a single product, to one, when it produces many products. It takes account, however, not only of the number of industries in which the firm is active but also of the distribution of its activity among those industries. Thus, a firm producing in a great number of industries but whose output is highly concentrated in only one of them will not be characterised as diversified according to this index. A firm whose output is equally divided among several industries, on the other hand, would be considered as diversified.

3. Wheeler and Mody (1992) illustrated numerous such factors.

4. The Country Assessment Service of Business International Inc., New York, constructs the BI database.

5. In algebraic terms, the effective rate of protection (ERP) is given as follows (Balassa, 1971; Corden, 1966):

$$ERP_j = (1 - S^n_{i=1} a_{ij}) / (1/i + t - S^n_{i=1} a_{ij}/1 + ti)$$

where $a_{ij}$ is the material input/output coefficient, i.e. the share of input $j$ in output $j$ at domestic process and

$t_j$ is the nominal *ad valorem* tariff rate or its equivalent (Heitger and Stehn, 1990, p. 7).

6. The revealed comparative advantage index (RCA) is defined as follows:

$$RCA_{(ij)} = (X_{ij} / X_i) / (X_{wj} / X_w)$$

where $X_{ij}$ = exports of item $i$ by country $j$; $X_i$ = total exports of country $j$; $X_{wj}$ = world exports of item $I$; and $X_w$ = total world exports. RCA ranges between zero and infinity, and values larger than one indicate that a country has comparative advantage in exporting item $i$ relative to competing countries in the world export market.

7. For the further elaboration of the differences in determinants across different types of FDI, the analysis will also employ a binomial probit model to accommodate dependent variables combined in two different modes.

8. In the estimation, the D/F/P and Newton algorithm methods will be employed for the multinomial and binomial probit models, using LIMDEP, a software package.

# Part Three

# The Impact of **FDI** on Exports

The impact of FDI on host countries has long attracted public attention. Initial concerns about whether FDI has a negative or positive impact on the balance of payments, debated in many countries, became the subject of several extensive studies. They applied methodology that varied from the analysis of firm–level transactions associated with particular investments to macro–level analysis of general–equilibrium effects. Most concluded that FDI has a positive effect on the balance of payments. Nevertheless, because the firm–level analyses covered only partial effects and the macro–level studies remained highly abstract, they remain subject to criticism and refutation.

Another major issue is whether FDI causes job losses. In the 1960s, labour unions in the United States claimed that FDI flows were associated with exports of jobs. This issue depends on an assumption about whether FDI replaces or substitutes for domestic investment. The AFL–CIO based its claims on the assumption that the jobs created by overseas affiliates simply displaced the equivalent number of domestic jobs. Business circles refuted this premise based on the opposite assumption. Numerous studies have recognised that the contrasting arguments are misplaced because they do not consider the indirect effects of establishing overseas affiliates. When indirect effects are included, the overall employment effects are marginally positive (UN, 1993). Labour unions in the United States raised this issue again in the NAFTA negotiations, insisting that Mexico would lure investments from the United States that would create job losses. Many studies have found these claims invalid, but the issue remains a major public concern based upon the common belief that FDI substitutes for domestic investments and exports. Recent debates about delocalisation in France, as well as Germany's concerns over the exodus of domestic industries to foreign countries, also closely related to the possible negative employment effects of FDI.

The effects of FDI on domestic investment and exports should be studied in the context of dynamic industrial adjustment, which is related to structural adjustment in the home economy. Structural changes occur continuously at home and abroad; some industries decline as others emerge and new comparative advantages are created. The ideas discussed in Part I support the positive effects of FDI on structural transformation, because firms can displace unsuitable industries or activities with more competitive ones by delocalising existing facilities to foreign countries. Kojima and Ozawa (1985) emphasised these effects for Japanese FDI in Asia, although Andersson (1995) found contradictory negative effects in Sweden. In fact, neither theoretical nor empirical research has yet covered all the aspects of these effects.

This Part concentrates on the possible impact of FDI on exports. Because all the questions concerning FDI interrelate, this analysis can partially explain other issues. Chapter 9 discusses substitution and complementary effects between FDI and exports and foreign and domestic investment, and reviews existing studies on the issue. Chapter 10 discusses their limitations and presents a possible alternative, which Chapter 11 uses for empirical analysis.

*Chapter 9*

# Causality between FDI and Exports

## Substitutes vs. Complements

A common notion holds that exports and FDI are alternative vehicles for serving foreign markets. It follows the logic that home–country industries can serve foreign markets either through exports or through foreign production. Firms can choose the more viable of these two options for penetrating foreign markets. This implies that the two modes are substitutable, or potentially so. This study has found, however, that market–proximity advantages join factor–proportion differences in influencing FDI. Yet they do not play an equivalent role in explaining international trade. The determinants of FDI thus are more complex than those of trade, which implies that FDI and exports are not mutually exclusive and thus not fully substitutable.

FDI enables firms to gain better access to foreign markets with the many advantages of local presence. Local production allows them to increase their market share in host countries, which mitigates the possible negative effects on exports of products supplied by foreign production. Nevertheless, it is clear that as their foreign production increases beyond certain levels, it can substitute for exports. Firms will be reluctant to push exports of items likely to compete with their foreign production in the same markets and to threaten the viability of their affiliates. Some factors, such as high transportation costs and tariff levels, which stimulate local production, also make exports less profitable.

More foreign production, on the other hand, generates exports of related capital equipment and intermediate goods. Over time, exports of intermediate goods will decrease as affiliates increase their local sourcing to adopt more flexible production systems or to meet local–content requirements, as discussed in Part One. Therefore, FDI can substitute for exports of these products from the home country in the long run. A Japanese study found that the export–generation effect increased for two years then gradually decreased, while export substitution and import diversion increased over time. The overall effect was positive for a certain period, but then turned negative (Japanese General Research Institute, 1990). Several surveys in Korea have found similar patterns (Korea Trade Association, 1994; MITI, Japan, 1990).

Apart from the relationship between goods produced abroad and those exported, foreign production can generally affect foreign demand for other products of investing firms. The brand images and expectations of reliable after–sales services that affiliates generate may often affect positively the firm's exports of such goods. A multi–product firm can benefit from these indirect effects, thereby mitigating the decreased exports caused by goods produced abroad.

The most important impact, however, lies in the *dynamic* positive effects of FDI on trade. They can stem from various factors. First, with their competitiveness strengthened through FDI, firms can increase their exports in the long run. Several factors allow investing firms to enhance their competitiveness over time. As discussed in Part One, they can divide their value chains and distribute them through FDI to optimal locations. The main motive for this is to reduce production costs, which in turn enables firms significantly to enhance their export competitiveness and thus improve their export performance.

Second, scale and scope economies can accrue not only in plants but also at the firm level. Fragmentation of value chains and specialisation of products can affect the magnitude of scale economies. Theoretically, a vertical, single–plant multinational can emerge to exploit maximum scale economies based on factor–proportion differences across countries. In the real world, however, scale economies arise through specialising in certain production segments or product differentiation. Firms can centralise segments intensive in capital and technology in the home or developed countries, while distributing labour–intensive segments in developing countries. Similarly, they can produce high–end or differentiated products in the home or developed countries while deploying low–end, standardised products in developing countries. In both cases, many subsidiaries can share management and R&D functions. These functional divisions and the sharing of support functions, along with product differentiation, enable firms to exploit larger scale and scope economies (Markusen, 1984).

Third, firms can enhance their competitiveness through transferring technology and experience between headquarters and subsidiaries, and among subsidiaries. Each subsidiary may have different advantages derived from the different characteristics of countries in which they operate. For instance, new software for factory automation can be developed more easily in a country where related education is well established, then transferred to headquarters and diffused to other affiliates. Many other factors generate positive dynamic effects on a firm's competitiveness as well. They include synergy and linkage effects as well as international networking (Porter, 1986). In general, these dynamic effects are not easy to measure.

A critic claims that there can be substitution effects on a parent's exports from the home country to third countries (Svensson, 1993). Although a subsidiary's exports to third countries may also attract imports of home–country intermediate goods to the host country, the notion that affiliates' exports create particularly strong substitution effects in third countries is convincing. The derived home–country exports of intermediate goods will be relatively small and thus cannot compensate for the negative effects. Some argue further that foreign production has some negative effect on exports from other domestic firms, but it is hard to estimate whether a firm's foreign production substitutes for or complements exports from other domestic competitors. Most applied methodologies are too vague to capture these effects and data unavailability makes firm–level analysis impossible. If any substitution effects do exist, other dynamic positive effects on the home and host economies can offset them. These dynamic effects can be expected in a macroeconomic perspective. As Kojima (1982) points out, the most viable option for a marginal industry is to establish foreign production to take advantage of cheap labour. Through delocating declining industries to other countries, home countries can invest more in emerging industries, which has positive effects on their structural adjustment.

Structural adjustment can also be achieved in the production process. Firms can change their production activities at home by delocating labour–intensive activities to foreign affiliates. Some firms with successful foreign operations tend to develop new activities and introduce new technologies in their home countries (Kojima and Ozawa, 1985). In addition to these positive effects on the home country, FDI can generate multiplier effects in the host economies. This study does not cover them, but home–country firms can indeed benefit from fostering the economic growth of host countries. In general, the dynamic positive effects together increase exports from the home country in the long run.

Another question regarding possible substitution or complementary effects of outward FDI concerns whether it displaces domestic investment in the home country. The answer depends on how that investment is financed. If it is financed through a cross–border capital flow, and if raising this capital crowds out home–country investment, then outward FDI would adversely affect domestic capital formation. Otherwise, there are only very few adverse impacts (UNCTAD, 1995). Feldstein (1994) estimates that about 20 per cent of US FDI is financed by cross–border capital flows from the United States, with an additional 18 per cent from retained earnings attributable to US investors. The rest is financed locally by foreign debt and equity. This estimate suggests that for each dollar of foreign assets acquired by US foreign affiliates, the US domestic capital stock is reduced by between 20 cents and 38 cents.

Individual firms may have a trade–off between FDI and domestic investment. If capital resources within a corporation are limited, FDI must have an adverse effect on domestic capital investment in the short term, but if investing firms face no financial constraints, there will be no substitution effects on investment in the home country. Few firms are free from financial constraints, so some adverse impacts on domestic investments are likely to arise. In this sense, FDI would admittedly have direct, negative effects on changes in the size of the indigenous capital stock. Indirectly, however, FDI can generate income flows, some of which are invested, or produce positive or negative multiplier effects for the country in question. Moreover, globalised firms can raise capital where it is least expensive, including internal financing, and use it where they expect highest rates of return. This more productive use of capital would enhance the industrial structure and improve the long–term economic performance of the home country.

In sum, it is hard to calculate the direct effects of FDI on exports, and it is even more difficult to find indirect effects and externalities. This implies that one cannot estimate the potential magnitude of substitution and complementary effects without knowing the specific characteristics of the investments in question (Markusen, 1991). Therefore, it is difficult to generalise that FDI is either a complement or a substitute for trade.

## Review of Major Studies

Many studies have attempted to find evidence of a relationship between overseas production and exports from home countries. They have developed various methodologies and approaches. Among them, the more business–oriented authors have tried to examine what would have happened in specific cases if investments abroad were not possible. In contrast, the econometric studies have sought an overall relationship between FDI and exports in large samples of firms or industries, using firm–level data or cross–industry data, which are available for only a few countries.

Reddaway et al. (1968) and Hufbauer and Adler (1968) found that the overall effect of outward FDI on the balance of payments is positive in the long run. They analysed payback periods, taking into account all possible cash flows including initial capital–equipment exports, components exports to subsidiaries and remittance of earnings from subsidiaries. The key factors in these studies are their assumptions about the effects on exports in the absence of the investment. Reddaway et al. explicitly assumed that in the absence of British foreign affiliates, their market would not have been serviced by British exports but rather by local or other foreign suppliers. Hufbauer and Adler, on the other hand, investigated several other possibilities, including exports from home countries. While export–displacement effects of investments rely on several sets of assumptions, their study includes the associated trade in products, intermediates and equipment in the calculations. The major contribution of these initial studies is that they identified the crucial importance of the assumptions.

A similar US study (Bergsten et al., 1978) found a positive relationship between outward FDI and the home–country balance of payments, using calculations based on related dividend, royalty and fee payments. This study also found that industries with low FDI show low export levels and vice versa. It further concluded that export performance tends to improve with increases in FDI up to a certain point, but beyond that point additional FDI does not appear to promote exports.

In response to the AFL–CIO's earlier claim that job losses result from the impact of runaway firms setting up labour–intensive operations in offshore locations, the US Tariff Commission analysed then–new data on the foreign operations of US firms. It found that employment gains generated from associated exports of equipment and parts, etc. and expansion of supporting non–production jobs would be large enough to offset possible job losses arising from production displacement effects (Hood and Young, 1979). In response to the latest concerns of the US labour unions, 23 studies have investigated the impact of FDI on employment. All except one have concluded that it has a positive effect resulting in the net increase of jobs (Madeuf, 1995).

Horst (1972) examined the relationship between US exports and foreign production through a cross–sectional regression analysis over industries and countries. The method he applied initially investigated the determinants of US exports and foreign production. The equations were then recalculated to derive the relationship between exports and subsidiary sales, holding all other variables constant. Using these equations, he found a highly significant positive relationship between US exports and foreign production. As noted above, however, Bergsten *et al.* (1978) found this relationship valid only up to a certain level of investment.

Lipsey and Weiss (1981) also examined the relationship between exports and FDI through a cross sectional analysis of exports of 14 manufacturing industries in the United States and 13 other developed countries to 44 foreign countries. They found that US affiliates' production tends to substitute for exports of foreigners, while foreign–owned affiliates' production tends to substitute for US exports. They included GDP and EEC membership as country characteristics. The most important missing variables, which affect both exports and foreign production, they admit, are host–country trade policies. They suspect that this omission biases their results toward showing substitution between exports and foreign production.

Besides these studies, several extensive empirical studies using Swedish firm–level data analyse the relationship between foreign production and home country–exports (e.g. Swedenborg, 1979, 1985; Blomström, *et al.*, 1988; Svensson, 1993). Among them, Swedenborg carried out the most detailed study. She contributed especially to the development of methodology by suggesting a two–stage–least–squares (2SLS) approach to resolve problems arising from simultaneity between FDI and exports. To avoid the problem, she initially estimated the level of production of Swedish affiliates in each host country and used this estimate as an exogenous variable in explaining parent exports (Swedenborg, 1979). From the 2SLS equations, she concluded that an increase in foreign production by one dollar increases the exports from the parent companies by 0.1 dollars.

Blomström *et al.* (1988) applied the same 2SLS and ordinary least squares (OLS) approach. The underlying analytical framework is a gravity model of trade, modified to explain the home country's exports to the host country as a function of affiliate production in the host country. The analysis confirmed, once again, that a complementary relationship exists between exports and affiliate sales. It found that both high initial levels of Swedish affiliate production in a country and increases in it associate positively with increases in Swedish exports to the country.

A study challenged these findings by pointing out that the earlier analyses did not include the effect of affiliates' production for export on the parents' exports to third countries (Svensson, 1993). It found that such affiliate exports reduce parent exports substantially[1], so much so that parent exports of intermediate goods to affiliates cannot compensate the substitution effect. Overall, foreign production has a negative effect on parent exports. Lipsey (1994), however, claimed that the effect on parent exports to third countries was included in his earlier analysis, which produced no negative effects. He argued that this contradiction might have arisen in equation formulation. Svensson normalised foreign production and exports across firms by their worldwide sales rather than by parent sales. This assumption, according to Lipsey, guarantees a negative coefficient for foreign production on home–country exports.

Brainard (1993) also applied 2SLS and at the same time introduced affiliate sales net of exports as a dependent variable to control for the simultaneity between exports and FDI. She examined the relationship between exports of US firms and sales of their foreign affiliates by analysing comprehensive industrial data covering bilateral activities between the United States and its major trading partners. She found that some factors, such as income levels and firm–specific advantages, increase both multinational sales and exports, but advertising intensity has no effect. Overall, she found a positive association between exports and affiliate sales.

Eaton and Tamura (1994) analysed Japanese and US bilateral trade flows and FDI positions with a sample of around 100 countries for 1985–1990. They applied a generalised gravity model that incorporated a Hecksher–Ohlin factor–intensity explanation for international trade. They took into account population, income, land–labour ratios, average levels of education and regions. The rationale behind this approach is that the intensity of bilateral trade and investment are affected primarily by not only their market sizes and the distance between the two countries, but also by differences in their relative factor endowments. Through the application of this model, they found that the country characteristics of population, per capita income, and resource endowments tend to have similar, if not identical, effects on the trade and FDI relationships. They maintained that these similarities suggest the existence of complementary effects between the trade and FDI (Brainard, 1993).

In sum, most studies have found a positive relationship between outward flows of FDI and exports from the home country, despite variations in methodologies and data. Some studies using firm–level data conclude that FDI has a complementary net effect on domestic exports. The advantages of market proximity were so strong that affiliates could gain greater market share than parent firms could by exporting from the home country only. Empirical analyses of FDI from other countries do not necessarily produce similar results, however. The questions remain open. Further studies using different data and approaches are needed.

**An Alternative Approach**

Despite numerous efforts, no single study so far has explained fully the dynamic impact of FDI on exports from home countries. Admittedly, it is nearly impossible to estimate the long–term dynamic effects. Yet a more specified analysis can produce some evidence of these effects. The discussion in Part One suggested that the impact of FDI on exports varies depending on its motives and purposes. FDI for foreign production, for example, has a more direct effect on exports than FDI for marketing and R&D. Similarly, the impact of foreign production for vertical integration differs from that for horizontal integration. Finding differences in the substitution, complementary or independent effects across different types of FDI on domestic investment and exports can reveal some insights into the dynamic effects.

The effects of FDI on domestic investment vary with the type of FDI. Some types of FDI are often associated with domestic expansion, while others occur along with partial or full disinvestment. In certain cases, FDI causes the replacement of domestic facilities. Theoretically, firms can construct an optimal combination of facility locations, sizes and production methods by weighing the relative importance of various factors. This optimisation inevitably brings about locational or technological changes in existing production facilities. The production literature clearly reveals this phenomenon.

"The construction of a new production facility by a firm requires that the firm make several interrelated decisions: how large the plant should be, what production method should be used, and where the facility should be located. With regard to the related decisions, differences in the elements across the value chain have focused the firm's decision on the spatial distribution for given production levels or techniques.

The extent of application of the flexible system, on the other hand, is closely related to the rapidly changing conditions of technology, marketing and sourcing. Furthermore, the flexible system has an impact on the decision not only for the relocation of the facilities but also for the redesign of the plants, and the replacement of the equipment. In any case, the increasing phenomenon of adopting new technology in the manufacturing and the information systems makes the interrelationships between the technological obsolescence, equipment replacement, and facility relocation substantially important." (Hurter and Martinich, 1989)

Thus, FDI is often associated with changes in existing production facilities and their spatial distribution. Firms can establish their foreign subsidiaries by redeploying domestic production facilities or by building new ones. Massive investments abroad, especially, will eventually associate with a shift in production capacity from the home country. Sometimes it results in the replacement or expansion of domestic facilities. Much depends on whether FDI stems from a voluntary decision for rational change or a non–voluntary reaction to an external factor.

Figure 9.1 shows the most probable matrix between different types of FDI and changes in domestic production facilities, and how vertical integration and delocalisation have contrasting domestic impacts. Vertical integration causes expansion, partly owing to acquisition of new resources and technologies. Delocalisation, on the other hand, induces partial or full domestic disinvestment. Horizontal expansion falls in between, but it can be voluntary or non–voluntary. The former has a more positive impact than the latter.

Figure 9.1. **Major Types of FDI and Changes in Domestic Production Facilities**

| | Vertical integration | Voluntary horizontal expansion | Non-voluntary horizontal expansion | Delocalisation |
|---|---|---|---|---|
| Full Disinvestment | | | | ▓ |
| Partial Disinvestment | | ▓ | | ▓ |
| No Change | | | ▓ | |
| Replacement | | ▓ | | |
| Expansion | ▓ | | | |

Note:     Shaded areas represent the probable impacts of each type of FDI on domestic investment.
Source:   Adapted by the author from concepts in Dicken (1992).

Expanded, these arguments explain differences in the impact on exports of various types of FDI. When firms invest abroad to exploit resources or technologies unavailable at home, this has, *prima facie*, no negative effects on domestic investment and exports. The firms concerned will frequently be part of a parent company's vertically integrated operations. Some studies insist that investments abroad in downstream industries generate more exports than upstream investment, which can be one reason why international vertical integration is biased toward downstream rather than upstream overseas investment (Eaton and Tamura, 1994).

FDI for voluntary horizontal expansions may have both complementary and substitution effects on exports. As discussed earlier, if investments and production transfers abroad are offensive moves or part of a global rationalisation of a multinational firm's activities, derived exports of intermediate goods can compensate some substitution effects on exports of final goods. Moreover, benefits of FDI derived from factor–cost saving and market proximity can expand trade in the long run. In contrast, if the decision to invest abroad responds to a threat to exports by either an upsurge in protectionism or intensified foreign competition, then foreign production likely will fully or partially displace domestic exports. If they do not invest abroad, of course, firms cannot continue exporting to their target markets and thus cannot maintain domestic production levels. FDI enables them to maintain their market shares in host countries, which would be lost otherwise, and a firm's adjustment subsequent to such investment tends to compensate for the initial displacement of home–country exports.

Figure 9.2 summarises this discussion. Because the overall impact of FDI on exports depends on the composition of FDI, it is risky to prejudge its substitution or complementary effects on exports without knowing that composition in terms of the different types of FDI. The different scenarios in the table reflect the offensive or defensive nature of the various types of outward FDI. Offensive FDI, including vertical integration and voluntary horizontal expansion, aims to increase market share or develop new markets. Defensive FDI, including delocalisation and non–voluntary horizontal expansion, tries to maintain current market share. The former can generate additional domestic exports of finished or intermediate goods but the latter cannot. Meanwhile, vertically or horizontally integrated production involves frequent flows of materials, semi–finished products and components. Exports of intermediate goods for final assembly abroad, however, depend crucially on host–country trade policies, and, at the extreme, delocalisation will likely bring about reverse exports (imports) to home countries (Madeuf, 1995).

Figure 9.2. **Major Types of FDI and Changes in Domestic Firm's Exports**

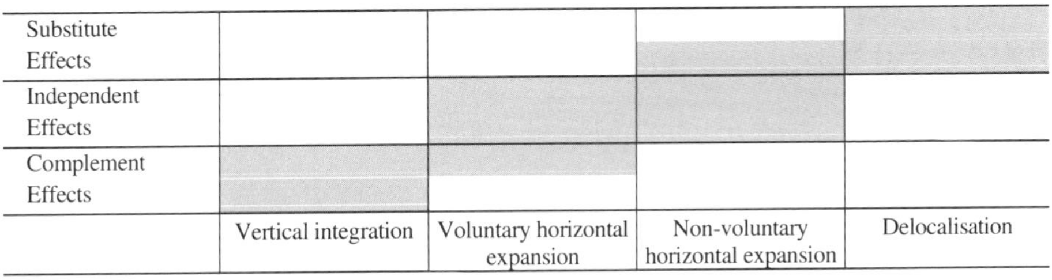

| | Vertical integration | Voluntary horizontal expansion | Non-voluntary horizontal expansion | Delocalisation |
|---|---|---|---|---|
| Substitute Effects | | | | |
| Independent Effects | | | | |
| Complement Effects | | | | |

*Note:* Shaded areas represent the possible effects of each type of foreign production on parent exports.
*Source:* Prepared by the author.

# Note

1.  The author states that 31 per cent of the production in affiliates of Swedish MNCs in the EC is exported to neighbouring countries.

# Analytical Framework

## Concepts

Most empirical studies based on firm–level data focus on parent firms' exports of finished and intermediate goods. It is a common notion that foreign production can replace parent exports of finished goods, but it does not simply substitute for such exports to the host country because, as discussed earlier, market proximity generates additional demand for locally produced items in the host market. Local production can be regarded as a guarantee for reliable, speedy delivery and for the continuity of after–sales services and repair. Therefore, it can shift the demand curve upward.

The establishment of a manufacturing subsidiary can generate positive dynamic effects on the parent's exports as well. It strengthens their competitiveness and shifts the supply curve for finished goods downward. Together, these effects can fully or partially offset the substitution effects on exports of finished goods to the host country. Exports to affiliates of parts and components can increase as well. Many firm–level analyses have found that increases in the parent's exports of intermediate and related products compensate lost exports of finished goods. Based on the analyses of the parent's exports of finished and intermediate goods, they conclude that FDI has positive effects on exports.

Yet these analyses cover only impacts on exports to host countries. In fact, manufacturing affiliates often serve third countries, especially other members of a trading bloc. These exports likely replace parent exports and those of other home–country firms to those countries. Therefore, the positive impact on the investing firm's exports to the host country does not necessarily secure a positive effect on all exports from the home country. A study found evidence supporting these arguments (Svensson, 1993).

Previous empirical studies also have not examined impacts on exports of parts and components to subsidiaries from domestic firms other than their parent firms. Most firms rely on outsourcing for supplies of parts and components, to reduce costs or avoid the risk of becoming heavily locked into their investments. Subcontracting is prevalent for outsourcing parts and components in the Korean electronic industry, and exports of subcontractors should be included in the analysis to capture the more comprehensive effects of FDI.

In short, a firm–level analysis should additionally include the effects not only on exports of finished goods to third countries but also those on intermediate goods exports by other domestic parts suppliers. While foreign production may have negative effects on exports of the home country to third countries, it may also have positive effects on the exports of other domestic parts suppliers. The net effect would be the sum of changes in the exports of a parent firm to the host and third countries, and in the exports of the domestic parts suppliers.

Figure 10.1 illustrates the possible impacts of FDI on trade flows. It depicts flows between the parent firm and its foreign subsidiary, and between its domestic parts suppliers and the subsidiary, as well as exports from the subsidiary to the home country and to the rest of world, and exports of the parent, subcontractors and other domestic firms to third countries. The total production of the subsidiary $(SQ)$ consists of its local sales $(SS_L)$, reverse exports to the home country $(SX_H)$ and exports to the rest of world $(SX_W)$, as depicted in the rectangles. The possible negative effects on exports of finished goods are illustrated with dotted circles while the potential positive effects on exports of intermediate goods are shown using bold circles. The normal circles represent exports on which the effects would be minimal.

Each component of affiliate output exerts different influences on home–country exports. $SS_L$ has direct impacts on parents' and other domestic firms' exports of finished goods to host countries $(P_iX_{FL}, RX_{FL})$, while $SQ$ stimulates exports of intermediate goods from parents, subcontractors, and other domestic firms $(P_iX_{NL}, CX_L, RX_{NW})$. $SX_W$, on the other hand, influences finished–goods exports of parents and other domestic firms to third countries $(P_iX_{FW}, RX_{FW})$. It would also have some indirect effects on home–country exports of intermediate goods to the rest of world, but they are excluded here because of difficulty in finding direct causality.

By definition:

(1) $SQ = SS_L + SX_W + SX_H$

(2) $PQ = PS_H + PX_{FL} + PX_{NL} + PX_{FW} + PX_{NW}$

(3) $CQ = CS_H + CX_L + CX_W$

(4) $RQ = RS_H + RX_{FL} + RX_{NL} + RX_{FW} + RX_{NW}$

(5) $SM_{NH} = PX_{NL} + CX_L + RX_{NL}$

(6) $HX = PX_{FL} + PX_{NL} + PX_{FW} + PX_{NW} + CX_L + CX_W + RX_{FL} + RX_{NL} + RX_{FW} + RX_{NW}$

## Figure 10.1. **Foreign Production and Flow of Associated Trade**

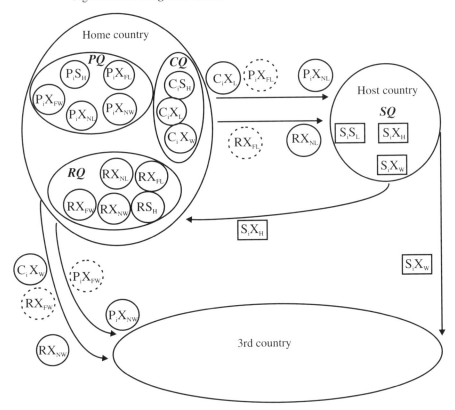

$S_iQ_k$    : Production of firm i's foreign subsidiary.

$S_iS_L$    : Local sales of firm i's foreign subsidiary.

$S_iX_W$    : Export sales to other than the host and home country from firm i's foreign subsidiary.

$S_iX_H$    : Reverse exports to the home country of firm i's foreign subsidiary.

$S_iM_{NH}$ : Imports of intermediate goods by firm i's foreign subsidiary from the home country.

$P_iS_H$    : Domestic sales by parent company of firm i.

$P_iX_{FL}$    : Exports of finished goods by parent company of firm i to the host country.

$P_iX_{FW}$    : Exports of finished goods by parent company of firm i to countries other than the host or home country.

$P_iX_{NL}$    : Exports of intermediate goods by parent company of firm i to the host country.

$P_iX_{NW}$    : Exports of intermediate goods by parent company of firm i to countries other than the host or home country.

$C_iS_H$    : Domestic sales of firm i's subcontractor.

$C_iX_L$    : Exports to the host country by firm i's subcontractor.

$C_iX_W$    : Exports to countries other than the host country by firm i's subcontractor.

$RS_H$    : Sales by other domestic firms to the home country.

$RX_{FL}$    : Exports of finished goods by other domestic firms to the host country.

$RX_{NL}$    : Exports of intermediate goods by other domestic firms to the host country.

$RX_{FW}$    : Exports of finished goods by other domestic firms to counties other than the host country.

$RX_{NW}$    : Export of intermediate goods by other domestic firms to countries other than the host country.

$HX$    : Exports by domestic firms.

## Model and Methodology

Figure 10.1 can serve as the basis for constructing a model to capture the impact of foreign production on exports from the home country. It suggests that local sales of foreign subsidiaries have an impact on exports to the host country by both their parents and other companies. The impact on other firms' exports of finished goods to host countries, however, is not only too ambiguous but also too complicated to be estimated statistically. The model is limited to analyses of the impact of subsidiaries' local sales on parents' exports to the host country. Similarly, exports of subsidiaries to the rest of the world would have effects on parents' and other firms' exports, but they also are too broad to be estimated statistically. This narrows the analysis further to embrace the impact on the parents' exports to affiliates' major export markets, mostly in trading blocs. The impact on exports of intermediate goods from the home country, on the other hand, can be observed from affiliates' derivative imports from the home country of raw materials and parts, which divides into imports from parents, their subcontractors and other domestic firms.

Equations *(10.1a)* and *(10.1b)* describe the model. Equation *(10.1b)* shows how exports of parent firms *(PX)* are affected by the production of foreign subsidiaries *(SQ)*. Both variables are normalised as annual growth rates[1]. $\partial SQ_{ijk}/SQ_{ijk}$ represents the most recent annual growth rate of foreign production of product $k$ by firm $i$ in market $j$, while $\partial PX_{ijk}/PX_{ijk}$ represents the latest annual growth rate of exports of product $k$ by firm $i$ to market $j$[2]. In the equations, $\alpha_I$ and $\beta_I$ are parameter vectors. $Z'_I$ is a vector of exogenous variables expected to influence foreign production in a host country, and $Z'_2$ is a vector of exogenous variables expected to affect exports from the home country to the host country. Therefore, $Z'_I$ and $Z'_2$ may explain the differences in the growth rates of exports and foreign production across firms, markets and products[3].

$$\partial SQ_{ijk}/SQ_{ijk} = \alpha_{0+} \alpha_I(\partial PX_{ijk}/PX_{ijk}) + Z'_I \alpha_2 + \epsilon_{ijk} \qquad (10.1a)$$

$$\partial PX_{ijk}/PX_{ijk} = \beta_0 + \beta_I (\partial SQ_{ijk}/SQ_{ijk}) + Z'_2 \beta_2 + \varepsilon_{ijk} \qquad (10.1b)$$

Equations *(10.1a)* and *(10.1b)* are classical forms of simultaneous equations. They contain the simultaneity problem inherently because foreign production and export patterns can be determined simultaneously. To avoid the problem, it is essential that the endogeneity of foreign production be removed. Among the many techniques for this, the present analysis employs estimation by the 2SLS method because, compared with OLS, it yields less biased estimates (Swedenborg, 1985).

The 2SLS method involves estimation in two steps. In the first, OLS is used to estimate the endogenous variable to explain another endogenous variable. In the second, the estimated value of this variable substitutes for its actual value in the equation. Using the estimated value of foreign production instead of its actual value eliminates the simultaneity problem[4]. Equation *(10.1b)* shows that the estimated value of foreign production replaces its actual value to become an explanatory variable additional to the existing exogenous variables.

The superiority of the model lies in the direct correspondence between exports and foreign production, specified by firm, market and product. The analysis earlier suggests specifying foreign–production and export–related variables that correspond more directly for the estimation of the causal relationship. For instance, exports of a certain item by an investing firm are affected more directly by local sales of its foreign subsidiary than by its production (Brainard, 1993). Similarly, exports of a subsidiary to a certain country would relate directly to the parent's exports to that country.

In order to estimate these multi–faceted effects more distinctively, then, the basic model should be modified and extended into several models. One can replace $\partial PX_{ijk}/PX_{ijk}$ with the growth rate of the parents' exports to the host country $(\partial PX_{FL}/PX_{FL})$ and $\partial SQ_{ijk}/SQ_{ijk}$ with the growth rate of local sales by the affiliate $(\partial SS_L/SS_L)$ to estimate the impact of the subsidiary's local sales on the parent's exports of finished goods. In the same manner, using the growth rate of derived exports of intermediate goods from the home country $(\partial SM_{NH}/SM_{NH})$ and the growth rate of production of foreign affiliates $(\partial SQ/SQ)$ can test for how foreign production affects exports of intermediate goods from the home country. Likewise, the causal relationship between the growth rate of reverse exports to the home country $(\partial SX_H/SX_H)$ and $\partial SQ/SQ$, and between the growth rate of parents' export to third countries $(\partial PX_W/PX_W)$ and the growth rate of export to third countries by foreign affiliates $(\partial SX_W/SX_W)$ can be tested empirically. Redefining the dependent and corresponding independent variables produces various sub–models as follows:

$$\partial PX_{FL}/PX_{FL} = \alpha_0 + \alpha_1(\partial SS_L/SS_L) + Z'_2\alpha_2 + \mu_{ijk} \qquad (10.2)$$

$$\partial SM_{NH}/SM_{NH} = \beta_0 + \beta_1(\partial SQ/SQ) + Z'_3\beta_2 + v_{ijk} \qquad (10.3)$$

$$\partial SX_H/SX_H = \delta_0 + \delta_1(\partial SQ/SQ) + Z'_4\delta_2 + \gamma_{ijk} \qquad (10.4)$$

$$\partial PX_W/PX_W = \kappa_0 + \kappa_1(\partial SX_W/SX_W) + Z'_5\kappa_2 + \sigma_{ijk} \qquad (10.5)$$

These equations can shed light on the following questions:

— To what extent do local sales of affiliates substitute for their parents' exports to the host country?

— How much does production of affiliates stimulate derived exports of intermediate goods from the home country?

— How much does production of affiliates bring about reverse exports (imports) to the home country?

— To what extent do affiliates' exports to third countries substitute for their parents' exports to the same countries?

One can approximate the net effect on exports by integrating the effects estimated by Equations *(10.2)*, *(10.3)* and *(10.5)* less the effect estimated by Equation *(10.4)*. Svensson (1993) claimed that most of the earlier studies found a positive effect on a parent's exports to the host country because they disregarded the effects on exports to third countries. He found that an affiliate's exports to third countries substantially reduce the parent's exports to those markets, which can be analysed by equation *(10.5)*, and concluded that the net effect is negative. This suggests that complementary effects on parents' exports of intermediate goods cannot compensate the possible substitution effect on parents' exports of finished goods to the rest of the world. However, Svensson did not include the potential complementary effect on other domestic firms' derivative exports of intermediate goods to the host countries and the negative effect of reverse exports to the home country. The expected total net effect, including the effects on other firms' exports of intermediate goods, should be positive.

The models specified in this section have basically two types of explanatory variables. The first (*FQEXIMs*) measures affiliates' production or trade. The second (*EGVRs*) is a set of exogenous variables. For *FQEXIMs*, Equations *(10.2)* and *(10.5)* require estimated values, while Equations *(10.3)* and *(10.4)* use actual values, depending on whether the simultaneity problem arises in each equation. The variables discussed in Part Three, on the other hand, may be good candidates for *EGVRs* that might affect affiliates' foreign production in a host country and exports from the home country to the host country.

Three other variables are included among the *EGVRs*: changes in *RCA* ($\partial RCA$), the length of time for foreign production (*AGE*) and a variable representing the degree of defensiveness or offensiveness of FDI *(DDO)*. The measure of $\partial RCA$ is the average annual change in *RCA* from 1990 to1994. The rationale for including it instead of *RCA* is to reflect the changing nature of comparative advantage over time. $\partial RCA$ must better correspond to some dependent variables because they too are measured by time differentials. *AGE* is the simple length of time for which each affiliate engaged in foreign production. It is a proxy for the accumulation of experience in foreign operations[5]. *DDO* measures different motives for FDI using a four–scale Likert survey, which gives higher values for offensive FDI and lower ones for defensive FDI. This study maintains that differences exist in the impact on exports of various types of FDI. *DDO* should enable an empirical test of this assertion.

All the exogenous variables mentioned above do not necessarily need to be included in each model. Rather, a set of independent variables will be specified in accordance with the characteristics of dependent and independent variables of each equation. Based on this logic and the actual specification of the model, the next section presents the set of explanatory variables to be included in each of the models.

## Data Observations and Descriptive Statistics of Variables

The database for the empirical analyses in this Part is constructed from trade and production statistics of the member firms of the Overseas Investment Council of the EIAK. The trade statistics of parents and their foreign affiliates were collected through questionnaires sent to all member firms, the same sample as that used in Part Three. Among the 188 production subsidiaries of 65 parent companies analysed there, only 145 subsidiaries of 55 parent companies provided trade and production statistics for 1994–1996. Most of the affiliates that did not provide trade data were newly established and thus had no such data.

The data are detailed enough to allow various cross–section analyses across firms, markets and products. They support two constructed data sets. The first is for Equations *(10.2)*, *(10.3)*, and *(10.4)*, based on disaggregated figures for parents, products manufactured by their affiliates and their host countries. The second serves Equation *(10.5)* with disaggregated data for parents, products manufactured by their affiliates, and the affiliates' third markets. Because some affiliates manufacture several items, the first data set raises the sample size to 204 observations. Each subsidiary manufactures 1.4 items on average. They include some affiliates not involved in local sales at all but exporting all of their production to third markets or to the home country. For several others, local sales did not change over the period. Consequently, 34.8 per cent of the $\partial SS_L/SS_L$ observations are zeros[6]. Similarly, several parent firms did not export finished goods to host countries and, in some cases, their exports to host countries remained static for the period. As a result, the portion of zeros in the observations for $\partial PX_{FL}/PX_{FL}$ reaches 57.4 per cent. $\partial SM_{NH}/SM_{NH}$ has about 11.8 per cent zeros, while the share of zeros in $\partial SX_H/SX_H$ reaches 70.6 per cent. Most subsidiaries import intermediate goods from the home country and a majority of them do not export to the home country.

The second data set has 192 observations. Some 107 affiliates (73.8 per cent of those in the sample) of 45 parent companies export their production to third markets. Around 16 per cent of the affiliates have no local sales and export exclusively to third markets. The relatively larger observations for the variable $\partial SX_W/SX_W$ imply that some affiliates serve multiple third markets. In fact, each affiliate serves around 1.8 major third markets on average. Since $SX_W$ denotes foreign affiliates' exports to their major markets, a zero value for $\partial SX_W/SX_W$ represents no change in exports to those markets. Therefore, the portion of zeros for $\partial SX_W/SX_W$ is relatively small, a meagre 5.2 per cent. Given the share of affiliates that serve third markets exclusively, the share of zeros for $\partial PX_W/PX_W$ is much higher, around 27.6 per cent.

Table 10.1 summarises the descriptive statistics for the foreign production and trade–related variables. The means of the former ($\partial SQ/SQ$, $\partial SS_L/SS_L$ and $\partial SX_W/SX_W$) are much larger than those of the latter ($\partial SX_H/SX_H$, $\partial PX_{FL}/PX_{FL}$ and $\partial PX_W/PX_W$), except for $\partial SM_{NH}/SM_{NH}$. The descriptive statistics show that the production and exports of affiliates grow much faster than exports from parent companies. Exceptionally, the import of intermediate goods by affiliates from the home country increased fairly rapidly. Also, the mean of $\partial PX_{FL}/PX_{FL}$ is much smaller than that of $\partial SQ/SQ$, which indicates that firms in the sample increased their foreign production much faster than their exports.

Table 10.1. **Descriptive Statistics for the Variables Related to Trade and Production**

|  | Variables | Mean | Standard Deviation |
|---|---|---|---|
| Data Set 1 | $\partial PX_{FL}/PX_{FL}$ | 0.08885 | 0.35114 |
|  | $\partial SM_{NH}/SM_{NH}$ | 0.45593 | 0.48989 |
|  | $\partial SX_H/SX_H$ | 0.13426 | 0.38165 |
|  | $\partial SS_L/SS_L$ | 0.38348 | 0.47030 |
|  | $\partial SQ/SQ$ | 0.51536 | 0.43942 |
| Data Set 2 | $\partial PX_W/PX_W$ | 0.05200 | 0.38438 |
|  | $\partial SX_W/SX_W$ | 0.44862 | 0.49937 |

Because the variables are measured by their growth rates, the absolute values of their effects can be obtained by multiplying the growth rate by the size of exports or production. Therefore, one needs to know the volume of exports or production in order to estimate the actual magnitude of the effects of foreign production on exports. Table 10.2 provides this information. In Data Set 1, the mean of $PX_{FL}$ is modest, even smaller than that of $SS_L$, while the mean of $SM_{NH}$ is surprisingly sizeable, larger than that of $PX_{FL}$. This implies that host countries are served more by foreign production than by exports. In Data Set 2, the mean of $SX_W$ is fairly high, equalling two–thirds of that of $PX_W$. This implies that the affiliates and their parent companies compete extensively in third markets. Also, the mean of $SX_W$ is even bigger than that of $SS_L$, which implies that affiliates place more emphasis on exports to third markets than on local sales. The sum of the means of $SS_L$, $SX_W$, and $SX_H$ is 36.27, which is slightly under 37.68, the mean of $SQ$, because the analysis of $SX_W$ does not include exports of foreign affiliates to minor third markets.

Table 10.2. **Average Trade and Production Volumes in the Sample**

|  |  | Observations | Mean | Standard Deviation |
|---|---|---|---|---|
| Sample for Data Set 1 | $SQ$ | 37.68 | 56.64 |
|  | $SS_L$ | 12.22 | 25.89 |
|  | $PX_{FL}$ | 8.90 | 33.79 |
|  | $SX_H$ | 3.07 | 6.54 |
|  | $SM_{NH}$ | 13.31 | 19.95 |
| Sample for Data Set 2 | $SX_W$ | 20.98 | 32.42 |
|  | $PX_W$ | 33.43 | 78.14 |

Each data set includes a corresponding set of exogenous variables (*EGVRs*), but all of the models do not necessarily employ the same set. Many exogenous variables should influence the dependent variables of particular export equations of others. For instance, a local–content requirement might exert a strong influence on $\partial SM_{NH}$ but it does not necessarily have equivalent effect on $\partial PX_{FL}$ and $\partial SX_H$. Other trade barriers of host countries do not have a direct relationship with $\partial PX_W$. Table 10.3 lists the explanatory variables to be included in each model and their expected signs in the estimation.

Table 10.3. **List of Explanatory Variables to be Included**

| Model | Dependent Variables | Explanatory Variables (Expected sign) | |
|---|---|---|---|
|  |  | *FQEXIMs* | *EGVRs* |
| 4.2 | $\partial PX_{FL}/PX_{FL}$ | $\partial SS_L/SS_L(-)$ | *RTP(?), dRCA(+), ECO(?), R&D(+), FMO(+), DDO(+)* |
| 4.3 | $\partial SM_{NH}/SM_{NH}$ | $\partial SQ/SQ(+)$ | *RTP(+), dRCA(?),R&D(?),DDO(?), AGE(-)* |
| 4.4 | $\partial SX_H/SX_H$ | $\partial SQ/SQ(+)$ | *MPX(-), RTP(-), ECO(?), R&D(?), FMO(-), DDO(?)* |
| 4.5 | $\partial PX_W/PX_W$ | $\partial SX_W/SX_W(-)$ | *ECO(+), FMO(?), RCA(?), dRCA(+), MSE(?)* |

118

# Notes

1. In some studies, e.g. Swedenborg (1979) and Svensson (1993), export and foreign production variables were normalised by parent production to represent the propensity for export and foreign production. The data by subsidiary used here, however, were constructed based on export and foreign production statistics measured by firm, market and product. In order to exploit these non–aggregated data fully, the annual growth rate of exports or foreign production is applied instead of the propensity to export or to produce overseas since most firms in the sample produce in multiple countries.

2. The instantaneous growth rate of variables, e.g. $SQ$, can be defined as $r_{SQ} = (\partial SQ / \partial t)/SQ$. Its annual growth rate, however, is measured as $\partial SQ_{ijk}/SQ_{ijk} = (SQ_t - SQ_{t-1})/SQ_{t-1}$.

3. The models require an instrumental variable that can identify the export equation in the 2SLS estimation. If the foreign production equation includes an instrumental variable in the first stage but the export equation excludes it in the second stage, one can identify the export equation. Therefore, $Z'_1$ should include some additional variables that do not appear in $Z'_2$.

4. The 2SLS–estimation also inherits problems such as multi–collinearity and auto–correlation. For details of problems of 2SLS, see Cumby *et al.* (1983).

5. *AGE* can be an instrumental variable since it has a relationship with foreign production but not with exports from the home country. For detail, see Swedenborg (1979).

6. Technically, a value of zero is assigned when sales or production volume remains zero for the period. In such cases, there obviously is no change, so this arbitrariness will not distort the result.

# Chapter 11

# FDI and Export Effects: Empirical Results

## Results of the Estimation

Table 11.1 reports the estimation of the effect of foreign production on exports of finished and intermediate goods to host countries. The first column (model *10.2*) gives the estimated effect of affiliates' local sales on parent exports of finished goods. The coefficient for $(\partial SS_L/SS_L)^\wedge$ is negative as predicted and significant at the one per cent level. This indicates that increases in local sales exert a negative impact on parents' exports of finished goods to host countries. When the growth rate of affiliates' local sales increases by one percentage point, parents' finished–goods exports to host countries drop, *ceteris paribus*, by 0.2826 per cent. Note that the coefficient does not represent the actual magnitude of the effect because the variables are measured by their growth rates and must be converted into absolute terms.

Table 11.1. **Estimated Results of Models *(10:2)* and *(10:3)***

| Model (method) | | Model *(10.2)* (2SLS) | Model *(10.3)* (OLS) |
|---|---|---|---|
| Dependent variable | | $\partial PX_{Fi}/PX_{Li}$ | $\partial SM_{NH}/SM_{NH}$ |
| Independent variable | | | |
| *Intercept* | | –0.7882*** | –0.2230** |
| *FQEXIMs* | $(\partial SS_L/SS_L)^\wedge$ | –0.2826*** | n.i. |
| | $\partial SQ/SQ$ | n.i. | 0.7850*** |
| *EGVRs* | *RTP* | 0.0121 | 0.0528*** |
| | $\partial RCA$ | 0.1432** | –0.0636 |
| | *ECO* | –0.0149 | n.i. |
| | *R&D* | 0.0188*** | –0.0110* |
| | *FMO* | 0.2720** | n.i. |
| | *DDO* | 0.2751*** | –0.0194 |
| | *AGE* | n.i. | –0.0315*** |
| DF | | 7 | 6 |
| $R^2$ | | 0.5050 | 0.6696 |
| F–value | | 28.570 | 66.538 |
| No. of observations | | 204 | 204 |

*Notes:*    ***, **, and * depict significance at the 1 per cent, 5 per cent, and 10 per cent levels, respectively.
n.i. = Not included in the regression.

The second column of the table, for model *(10.3)*, shows the estimated effect of foreign production on exports of intermediate goods from the home country. The coefficient for $\partial SQ/SQ$ is positive and significant at the one per cent level. This verifies that increased foreign production attracts imports of intermediate goods from the home country and suggests that the effect is substantial. A one percentage–point increase in foreign production leads to a 0.7850 per cent increase in home–country exports of intermediate goods. The size of the effect may reflect the comprehensive measurement of derived exports of intermediate goods from domestic firms, including parents' subcontractors, which previous empirical studies have not taken into account.

In model *(10.2)*, among other exogenous variables, the coefficients for *DDO* and *R&D* are significant at the one per cent level, while those for $\partial RCA$ and *FMO* are significant at the five per cent level. All are positively signed as predicted, meaning that they are positively related to the growth rate of parents' exports of finished goods to host countries. The positive and highly significant coefficient for *DDO* deserves special attention, which it receives in the next section.

In model *(10.3)*, the coefficients for *RTP* and *AGE* are significant at the one per cent level and that for *R&D* is significant at the ten per cent level. *RTP* is positively signed but *R&D* and *AGE* are negatively signed. This contradictory relationship may arise because assembly subsidiaries established to circumvent trade barriers have a tendency to import more intermediate goods from the home country. It also suggests that firms with high *R&D* intensity tend to rely more on local sourcing, while those with low *R&D* intensity are apt to depend more on sourcing from the home country.

The negative and highly significant coefficient on *AGE* represents the changing pattern in outsourcing of foreign affiliates over time. When an MNC establishes a production affiliate abroad, domestic firms, including parents and their subcontractors in the home country, may be able to increase their exports of intermediate goods to the host country, but this effect cannot necessarily be sustained over time. The outsourcing patterns of subsidiaries evolve differently in accordance with the trade policies of host countries. Suppliers of subsidiaries facing local–content requirements can evolve in two directions that eventually affect the subcontracting systems. Either suppliers in the host countries replace domestic subcontractors, or they follow their contractors by investing in the host countries, as evidenced by FDI from Japan and Korea.

In countries without significant trade barriers, investing firms are likely to increase global sourcing in response to intensified global competition. Some firms come to rely in part on local parts suppliers when transportation costs remain significant and flexibility in supply becomes critical. The production of bulky parts will likely shift first to local markets owing to high transportation costs, while non–competitive parts may become subject to outsourcing. The production of competitive and core parts may well remain in home markets as long as host countries do not impose any special restrictive trade policies. When they do impose such policies or when affiliates adopt new production technologies, production of competitive and core parts shifts to host countries, as discussed in Part Two. In assembly industries such as electronics and transportation equipment, large firms encourage their domestic subcontractors, mostly SMEs, to invest near their foreign assembly lines in order to secure stable and efficient sourcing or to meet restrictive local–content rules.

Table 11.2 presents the estimation results for models *(10.4)* and *(10.5)*. The first column (model *10.4*) shows the estimated effects of foreign production on the reverse exports of products manufactured by foreign affiliates to the home country. The positive coefficient on $\partial SQ/SQ$ verifies that the expanded production brings about an increase in reverse exports. When the growth rate of production by foreign affiliates increases by one percentage point, that of reverse exports increases by 0.2360 per cent. The impact is minor in absolute terms, however, because the mean value of $SQ$ is much higher than that of $SX_H$. The second column (model *10.5*) reveals the effects of foreign production destined for third countries on parents' exports of finished goods to the same markets. Affiliates' exports to third countries, as expected, exert a negative impact on parents' exports, but the relationship is weak, not statistically significant and therefore practically negligible.

Table 11.2. **Estimated Results of Models *(10.4)* and *(10.5)***

| Model (method) | | Model *(10.4)* (OLS) | Model *(10.5)* (2SLS) |
|---|---|---|---|
| Dependent variable | | $\partial SX_i/SX_H$ | $\partial PX_i/PX_W$ |
| Independent variable | | | |
| *Intercept* | | 0.5502*** | 0.4184** |
| FQEXIMs | $\partial SQ/SQ$ | 0.2360*** | n.i. |
| | $(\partial SX_W/SX_W)$ ^ | n.i. | –0.2284E–04 |
| EGVRs | *MPX* | –0.1136*** | n.i. |
| | *RTP* | –0.0645*** | n.i. |
| | *ECO* | –0.0498** | 0.0357** |
| | *R&D* | 0.0103 | n.i. |
| | *FMO* | –0.5337*** | –0.4557** |
| | *DDO* | 0.0128 | n.i. |
| | *RCA* | n.i. | –0.0185* |
| | $\partial RCA$ | n.i. | 0.0941 |
| | *MSZ* | n.i. | –0.0262 |
| DF | | 7 | 6 |
| $R^2$ | | 0.2455 | 0.0909 |
| F–value | | 9.112 | 3.082 |
| No. of observations | | 204 | 192 |

*Notes:*    ***, **, and * depict significance at the 1 per cent, 5 per cent, and 10 per cent levels, respectively.
n.i. = not included in the regression as presented in Table 10.3.

In model *(10.4)*, the coefficients for *MPX, RTP,* and *FMO* are significant at the one per cent level, while *ECO* is significant at the five per cent level. All are negatively signed. The negative coefficients for *MPX* and *RTP* imply that foreign affiliates established to exploit market proximity and avoid trade friction are less interested in reverse exporting. The coefficients for *ECO* and *FMO*, on the other hand, suggest that small and medium-size firms, depending heavily on their home markets, are more active in reverse exports.

Model *(10.5)* has no exogenous variables significant at the one per cent level. Only two variables, *ECO* and *FMO,* are significant at the five percent level, and *RCA* is significant at the ten percent level. *FMO* and *RCA* are negatively signed while *ECO* is positively signed. The remaining explanatory variables, including $\partial SX_W/SX_W$, are not statistically significant. These vague relationships between dependent and explanatory variables cause poor performance of the equation, as indicated by the negligible $R^2$ value and F statistics.

Table 11.3 summarises the results of the regressions and presents the estimated effects in absolute terms. Because each coefficient is measured as a ratio of growth rates, it can be interpreted as an elasticity, and one can estimate what the corresponding coefficient would have been, had the regression been run on the same variables measured in absolute terms. This is done by multiplying the estimated coefficients by the means of the denominators for the dependent variables and dividing the result by the means of the denominators for the explanatory variables (*FQEXIMs*). For instance, the absolute value of the effect of local sales on parents' exports of finished goods comes from multiplying the coefficient for $(\partial SS_L/SS_L)^\wedge$ by the mean of $PX_{FL}$ and subsequently dividing it by the mean of $SS_L$.[1]

Table 11.3. **Magnitude of Effects by Analysed Variables**

| Dependent variable | Independent variable | Coefficient | Value in absolute terms |
|---|---|---|---|
| $\partial PX_{FL}/PX_{FL}$ | $(\partial SS_L/SS_L)^\wedge$ | –0.2826 | –0.2058 |
| $\partial SM_{NH}/SM_{NH}$ | $\partial SQ/SQ$ | +0.7850 | 0.2731 |
| $\partial SX_H/SX_H^{[1]}$ | $\partial SQ/SQ$ | +0.2360 | 0.0192 |
| $\partial PX_W/PX_W$ | $(\partial SX_W/SX_W)^\wedge$ | –0.2284E–04 | –0.3639E–04 |

*Note:*    In summing up the net effect, although the coefficient for $\partial SX_H/SX_H$ is positive, one should subtract effects on reverse exports as discussed in Chapter 10.

The table shows that when local sales of affiliates increase by one dollar, the parent's exports of finished goods decrease by 0.2058 dollars. An increase in foreign production by one dollar stimulates imports of intermediate goods from the home country by 0.2731 dollars, and increases reverse exports by 0.0192 dollars. When affiliates' exports to third countries increase by one dollar, the parents' exports to third countries decrease, but negligibly.

Summing these partial effects gives the net effect although, admittedly, the simple sum is not necessarily accurate because each coefficient is measured by different explanatory variables (*FQEXIMs*), as the table shows. The effects on parent exports to host countries and third countries, for example, are measured by the respective effects of affiliates' local sales and exports to third countries. Nevertheless, because the *FQEXIMs* tend to increase together with foreign production, the sum of these estimations can approximate the net effect. Therefore, based on Table 11.3, that effect appears as marginally positive.

To sum up, the equations presented provide strong evidence that the positive effect on derived exports of intermediate goods to host countries is strong enough to compensate for the negative effects on parents' exports of finished goods. The equation for estimating effects on exports to third countries, on the other hand, performs poorly and produces very weak negative effects. The effects on reverse exports to the home country are significantly positive but become negligible when the value of the coefficient is converted to absolute terms. Taken together, these results suggest that foreign production has a positive impact on exports from the home country. The approximation of net effects generally coincides with the direction and magnitude of the overall effect on parents' exports. Note, however, that the calculated effects have validity only for foreign production of the Korean electronics industry in 1996. The export effect is not consistent over time and across different types of FDI as indicated by the highly significant effects of *DDO* and *AGE* in some models.

## Differences in the Effects on Exports across Different Types of FDI

Chapter 9 maintained that there must be differences in the impact of foreign production on exports across various types of foreign production. Offensive foreign production, including vertical integration and voluntary horizontal expansion, should generate additional exports of finished goods from the home country because it aims to increase market share or develop new markets. Defensive foreign production, on the other hand, including delocalisation and non–voluntary horizontal expansion, aims at maintaining current market share through foreign production and thus is expected to substitute for exports from home countries. The positive and highly significant coefficient for *DDO,* in model *(10.2)* (Table 11.1), supports this argument. It shows that offensive foreign production is inclined to associate with an increase in exports of finished goods from the home country, while defensive foreign production has a tendency to accompany a decrease in such exports.

More specifically, the hypothesis is that foreign production in categories I and III has a positive impact on home–country exports, while that in categories II and IV has a neutral or negative impact on parents' exports, as shown in Table 11.4. Because the total effect is the simple sum of these different effects, it depends on the weights of the different types of foreign production. Countries that have large shares of offensive foreign production can increase exports through FDI, while those which have large shares of defensive foreign production may face declines in exports.

To test this hypothesis empirically, one can divide the sample to accord with the different foreign production categories and analyse variations in the effect on exports across the sub–samples. The grouping of the samples involves subjective judgements, however. To avoid this problem, the sample here is divided into two separate sub–samples bisected by firm size, location and product, respectively. This produces three pairs of two separate sub–samples: subsidiaries of conglomerates and SMEs;

subsidiaries in developed and developing countries; and subsidiaries manufacturing finished goods and intermediate goods. If the regression results provide some variations in the effect on exports across the sub–samples, the hypothesis has indirect support. These results are displayed in Tables 11.4 through 11.7.

As the first experiment, 2SLS regressions apply model *(10.2)* to each sub–sample (Table 11.4). Substitution effects prevail in the regression for conglomerates while complementarity effects appear in the regression for SMEs. In addition, foreign production in developed countries substitutes more for parents' exports than that in developing countries. The high substitution effects for conglomerates' production in developed countries may be due to non–voluntary investment aimed at avoiding trade frictions. Substitution effects from production in developing countries may be due to delocalisation. The coefficient for *DDO* is consistently positive and highly significant across the sub–samples.

In the OLS regression results obtained by applying model *(10.3)* to each sub–sample (Table 11.5), the positive effects on foreign affiliates' imports of intermediate goods are consistent across the sub–samples, but some variations appear in the magnitudes across the sub–samples. The effects on derived exports of intermediate goods from the home country are stronger for SMEs than for conglomerates. Similarly, developed countries have a somewhat stronger effect than developing countries on derived exports of intermediate goods. This might occur because production subsidiaries established by SMEs rely more on domestic parts suppliers, and assembly subsidiaries established in developed countries import parts from the home country as much as possible. The coefficients for *AGE* are negative across all sub–samples, although some variations in its magnitudes exist across the sub–samples.

Table 11.6 presents the results of the OLS regression obtained by applying model *(10.4)* to each sub–sample. The coefficient for $\partial SQ/SQ$ is positive for developing countries but negative for developed countries. In the remaining sub–samples, the coefficients are all positive, but the effects are stronger for SMEs and intermediate goods than for conglomerates and finished goods. This implies that SMEs' foreign production of intermediate goods in developing countries tends to bring about more reverse exports than conglomerates' foreign production of finished goods in developed countries. Delocalisation is pursued mostly by SMEs producing intermediate goods in developing countries, which results in substantial reverse exports.

Finally, in 2SLS regressions applying model *(10.5)* to each sub–sample (Table 11.7), notable differences appear across the sub–samples in the effects on exports to third countries. The coefficient for $(\partial SX_w/SX_w)^{\wedge}$ is negative for conglomerates and finished goods, but the sub–samples for SMEs and intermediate goods have positive coefficients. This suggests that conglomerates' foreign production of finished goods destined to third markets has substitution effects, but, in contrast, SMEs' foreign production of intermediate goods destined for third markets has complementary effects.

Overall, the direction and magnitude of the coefficients on variables representing foreign affiliates' production and trade coincide with the earlier arguments in this study. In addition to the positive and significant coefficient on *DDO*, the results just

Table 11.4. **Differences in the Effects on Parents' Exports of Finished Goods**

| Dependent variable | | | | Independent variable | | | | | | | |
|---|---|---|---|---|---|---|---|---|---|---|---|
| $\partial PX_{tt}/PX_{tt}$ | Constant | $\delta SS_t/SS_t$ | RTP | dRCA | ECO | R&D | FMO | DDO | $R^2$ | F–value | No. of obs. |
| SMEs | 0.3975*** | 0.1075 | -0.0491* | 0.0842 | n.i. | 0.4061E-03 | 0.0441 | 0.2033*** | 0.5955 | 18.157 | 81 |
| Conglomerates | -1.4331*** | -0.3679*** | 0.0335 | 0.1102 | n.i. | 0.0301*** | 0.8788*** | 0.2857*** | 0.5356 | 22.297 | 123 |
| Developed countries | -1.0327*** | -0.3700*** | 0.0134 | -0.0384 | 0.0210 | 0.0148 | 0.3408 | 0.2857*** | 0.5320 | 68.207 | 50 |
| Developing countries | 0.7211*** | 0.2408* | 0.0064 | 0.1679*** | -0.0187 | 0.0207*** | 0.2332* | 0.2675*** | 0.5459 | 25.077 | 154 |

*Notes:* Obtained through 2SLS regression with model (*10:2*). Coefficients marked ***, ** and * are significant at the 1, 5 and 10 per cent levels respectively.
n.i. = Not included in the regression as presented in Table 10.3.

Table 11.5. **Differences in the Effects on Foreign Affiliates' Imports of Intermediate Goods**

| Dependent variable | | | | Independent variable | | | | | | | |
|---|---|---|---|---|---|---|---|---|---|---|---|
| $\delta SM_{NH}/SM_{NH}$ | Constant | $\delta RQ/SQ$ | RTP | dRCA | R&D | AGE | DDO | $R^2$ | F–value | No. of obs. |
| SMEs | 0.0993 | 0.8200*** | 0.0809** | -0.0103 | -0.0038 | -0.0208* | -0.0020 | 0.7111 | 30.359 | 81 |
| Conglomerates | 0.3062** | 0.7633*** | 0.0513*** | -0.1333 | -0.0112* | -0.0440*** | -0.0303 | 0.6028 | 29.345 | 123 |
| Developed countries | -0.1032 | 0.8812*** | 0.0510 | -0.0077 | 0.2265E-03 | -0.0206 | 0.0349 | 0.7806 | 25.493 | 50 |
| Developing countries | 0.3013*** | 0.7591*** | 0.0590*** | -0.0681 | -0.0138*** | -0.0339*** | -0.0353 | 0.6373 | 43.041 | 154 |

*Note:* Obtained through OLS regression with model (*10:3*). Coefficients marked ***, ** and * are significant at the 1, 5 and 10 per cent levels respectively.

Table 11.6. **Differences in the Effects on Reverse Exports to the Home Country**

| Dependent variable | Constant | Independent variable | | | | | | | R² | F-value | No. of obs. |
|---|---|---|---|---|---|---|---|---|---|---|---|
| $\delta X_H/SX_H$ | | $\delta Q/SQ$ | MPX | RTP | ECO | R&D | FMO | DDO | | | |
| SMEs | 0.1266 | 0.3492*** | -0.0896** | 0.0441 | n.i. | 0.0302** | -0.3346** | 0.0916** | 0.4061 | 84.347 | 81 |
| Conglomerates | 1.4044*** | 0.1391* | -0.1059*** | -0.0881*** | n.i. | -0.0013 | -0.9477*** | -0.0274 | 0.3223 | 9.193 | 123 |
| Developed countries | 0.7137* | -0.0286 | -0.2160*** | 0.0954* | -0.0059 | 0.0382* | -0.6571 | 0.0859* | 0.2639 | 2.151 | 50 |
| Developing countries | 0.5085*** | 0.2867*** | -0.0806** | -0.0982*** | 0.0723*** | 0.0053 | -0.5893*** | 0.0047 | 0.3346 | 10.490 | 154 |
| Finished goods | 0.7575*** | 0.1183* | -0.0978*** | -0.0188 | 0.0167 | 0.0151** | -0.9347*** | 0.0101 | 0.3369 | 6.678 | 100 |
| Intermediate goods | 0.3012 | 0.2732** | -0.0190 | -0.0754** | 0.0627** | -0.0123 | -0.3875 | 0.0159 | 0.1905 | 3.228 | 104 |

*Notes:* Obtained through OLS regression with model (10.4). Coefficients marked ***, ** and * are significant at the 1, 5 and 10 per cent levels respectively.
n.i. = Not included in the regression as presented in Table 10.3.

Table 11.7. **Differences in the Effects on Exports to Third Countries**

| Dependent variable | Constant | Independent variable | | | | | | R² | F-value | No. of obs. |
|---|---|---|---|---|---|---|---|---|---|---|
| $\delta PX_w/PX_w$ | | $\delta X_w/SX_w$ | MSZ | RCA | $\delta RCA$ | ECO | FMO | | | |
| SMEs | 0.2274 | 0.8105*** | 0.0023 | 0.0174 | 0.1087 | n.a. | -0.7218*** | 0.1804 | 33.468 | 82 |
| Conglomerates | 0.7609*** | -0.7136E-04 | -0.0831 | -0.0220* | 0.1868 | n.a. | -0.3910 | 0.0858 | 1.952 | 110 |
| Developed countries | 0.4140** | -0.4649E-04 | -0.0417 | -0.0108 | 0.0766 | 0.0212 | -0.3194 | 0.0729 | 1.639 | 132 |
| Developing countries | 0.6228* | -0.4266 | -0.1363 | -0.0598** | 0.1484 | 0.1776*** | -0.7116** | 0.3080 | 3.932 | 60 |
| Finished goods | 0.8552*** | 0.5976E-03** | -0.1627*** | -0.0109 | 0.2264** | 0.0407 | -0.5279*** | 0.2814 | 6.331 | 104 |
| Intermediate goods | 0.3052 | 0.2253E-03 | 0.0316 | -0.0062 | -0.0294 | -0.0561** | -0.6522* | 0.0917 | 1.362 | 88 |

*Notes:* Obtained through 2SLS regression with model (10.5). Coefficients marked ***, ** and * are significant at the 1, 5 and 10 per cent levels respectively.
n.i. = Not included in the regression as presented in Table 10.3.

described further confirm that different types of FDI tend to associate with different substitution and complementarity effects on exports from the home country. Incorporating these findings with the previous findings on major determinants of each type of FDI, the following conclusions emerge:

— First, substitution effects on parent exports arise in conglomerates' foreign production destined for local sale, while complementarity effects on parent exports appear in SMEs' foreign production for local sale. Part Two found that restrictive trade policies of host countries are the most influential determinant of conglomerates' foreign production of finished goods in developed countries, while low labour costs are the most critical factor attracting SMEs to produce intermediate goods in developing countries. Thus, conglomerates' foreign production of finished goods in developed countries, aimed at avoiding trade friction, exerts an adverse impact on parents' exports to host countries. SMEs' foreign production of intermediate goods in developing countries, aimed at exploiting low labour costs, exerts marginally positive effects on parents' exports to the host countries.

— Second, the effects on affiliates' imports of intermediate goods from the home country are consistently positive and significant across different types of FDI. They cannot be sustained for long periods, however, because derived exports of intermediate goods will diminish over time. Most of Korean firms' foreign production has been established recently, so the positive effect on the derived exports of intermediate goods is predominant and strong enough to compensate for the possible negative effects on parents' exports of finished goods to host countries. As a result, the net effect of foreign production on Korean exports is convincingly positive.

— Third, SMEs' foreign production of intermediate goods in developing countries has a tendency to associate with reverse exports to the home country. A substantial portion of such foreign production involves delocalisation. Hence, delocalisation, especially by SMEs to make intermediate goods abroad, increases reverse exports.

— Finally, conglomerates' foreign production of finished goods destined for third markets has weak, statistically insignificant adverse effects on exports from the home country to those markets, while such negative effects do not appear at all in the SMEs' foreign production of intermediate goods destined for third markets.

The results of the regressions applying the models to each sub–sample largely confirm earlier arguments. Foreign production exerts influences on complementary and substitute exports, in opposite directions. Because the complementarity effects of derived imports of intermediate goods prevail over the possible substitution effects on the exports of finished goods, the net effect is marginally positive. This supports the hypothesis that positive dynamic effects may mitigate substitution. The argument that the impact on exports differs for different types of foreign production is also empirically proven. The regression results indirectly show that vertical integration and voluntary expansion have positive impacts on home–country exports, while non–voluntary expansion and delocalisation have neutral or negative impacts on them.

The findings have strong policy implications as well. Most developing countries neglect the strong linkages between FDI and trade. They have rarely noted the dynamic effects whereby FDI can generate exports from home countries. Instead, they have been preoccupied with the notion that foreign production brings about substitution and thus reduces home–country exports. Accordingly, many of them have simultaneously maintained restrictive outward–FDI policies and pursued trade–promotion policies. Korean experience suggests that these countries do not need to discourage outbound FDI to protect their exports. Moreover, they should commit more to offensive rather than defensive FDI, to enhance their exports. This does not necessarily argue that home countries should adopt discriminatory incentives for offensive FDI, however. Rather, they should try to eliminate restrictive host–country trade policies, which adversely affect not only trade but also FDI flows. Such policies often extort commercially unviable FDI from developing countries, which generates a further negative impact on exports from the home country. This eventually distorts the distribution of resources (see OECD, 1989, for example). Governments and international organisations should work together to eliminate such restrictions.

# Note

1.  In algebraic terms, it can be represented as $\partial PX_{FL}/\partial SS_L = [(\partial PX_{FL}/PX_{FL})/(\partial SS_L/SS_L)]$ x $(PX_{FL}/SS_L)$.

*Chapter 12*

# Conclusions

This study began with a suggested conceptual framework to illustrate the optimal deployment of corporate functions based on international differences in factor proportions and on the need for market proximity across segments of the value chain. It noted how distinctive and different attributes of the various segments affect the spatial distribution of firms' functions and subsequently determine a sequence in the deployment of the value chain. This sequence can change with changes in external or internal factors, such as new trade policies or production technologies. Restrictive trade policies of major trading partners as well as incentives for FDI have significant spatial effects on value chain deployment. The application of new production technology can change factor intensity in manufacturing and thus affect the optimal location of production facilities for the globalisation of developing country firms.

In a broader context, firms distribute their value chains in response to changing technological and competitive environments, which determine competitive and comparative advantages. The study categorises and characterises different types of FDI by the different market and technology conditions in which firms invest abroad. In this process, it formulates explicit hypotheses regarding the determinants and effects of FDI, which differ across different types of FDI. Regression analysis to test these hypotheses for firms in the Korean electronics industry finds that their decision making to choose entry modes is affected by various factors related to advantages of market proximity as well as differences in factor proportions. The regression results give further evidence that factors affecting these decisions differ across different sub–groups categorised by attributes specific to firms, host countries and products.

In order to test empirically the hypotheses on different determinants of FDI for the globalisation of corporate activities, the study proposed a comprehensive dynamic framework for investment decision making by developing country firms. Following this framework, it specified an econometric model representing the functional relationship between modes of subsidiaries and three sets of exogenous variables, namely the factors specific to firms, markets and products. The database was constructed based on comprehensive firm–level data for Korean electronics firms. It provides information on the exogenous variables and four different modes of subsidiaries: marketing, production and R&D subsidiaries, and regional headquarters. The major findings of the statistical analysis using this database are as follows.

—   First, preliminary analyses with the chi–square test found significant differences in entry modes across firms, markets and products. Using Spearman's formula for rank correlation, it also found differences in the order of establishing the various modes of subsidiaries across regions. This supports the argument that market–specific factors might be critical in the distribution of firms' value chains.

—   Second, a statistical test of the modal choices, applying a multinomial probit model to cross–sectional data, revealed that the exogenous variables together explained fairly well Korean firms' behaviour regarding those choices. Most of the employed variables except the two product–specific variables were statistically significant, and all significant variables except economic concentration were positively signed as predicted.

—   Third, to test the hypothesis of differences in determinants across different types of FDI, the analysis divided the sample into three pairs of sub–samples bisected by firm size, location and products. Regressions applying the models to these sub–samples found that SMEs respond more sensitively to labour–cost differentials than do conglomerates, while conglomerates are more vulnerable to protective trade measures than SMEs. These results further confirmed that investment in developed countries is strongly triggered by restrictive trade measures, while low labour costs mainly motivate investment in developing countries. Restrictive trade measures are also the most influential factor attracting FDI for manufacturing finished goods, mostly consumer electronics, while low labour costs are most critical for FDI to manufacture intermediate goods.

Viewing the evidence as a whole, one can conclude that restrictive trade measures are the most critical determinant of FDI by conglomerates in developed countries in finished goods, while low labour costs have the most influence on FDI by SMEs in developing countries in intermediate goods. These statistical findings indirectly support the hypothesis that different types of FDI have different critical determinants.

Chapter 11 found some empirical evidence on the impact of FDI on exports from the home countries. It used a dynamic framework that covers not only the causal relationship between local sales in and parents' exports to host countries, but also the effects of foreign production on exports of intermediate goods to foreign subsidiaries. The framework further included the potential impact of subsidiary exports to third markets on parents' exports to those markets. Based on the framework, the analysis specified related models representing the relationship between directly corresponding variables. The trade and production statistics for Korean electronics firms were detailed enough to allow various cross–sectional analyses.

The regression results evidenced that the positive effects on the derived exports of intermediate goods to host countries are strong enough to compensate for the negative effects on parents' exports of finished goods. The equation for estimating effects on exports to third countries, on the other hand, performed poorly and produced very weak negative effects. The effects on reverse exports to the home country were significantly positive but became negligible when the value of the coefficient was converted to absolute terms.

The approximation of net effects was marginally positive. This supported the hypothesis that dynamic positive effects can offset the possible substitution effects. Foreign production exerts influences on complementary and substitute exports in opposite directions, but, because the complementarity effects of derived imports of intermediate goods prevail over substitution effects on exports of finished goods, the net effect of FDI on exports from the home country becomes marginally positive.

From the hypothesis of significant differences in impact across different types of FDI, the study argued that the offensive or defensive nature of the various types of outward FDI determines their effects on exports. This argument follows the logic that offensive FDI, including vertical integration and voluntary horizontal expansion, aims to increase market share or develop new markets. Defensive FDI, including delocalisation and non–voluntary horizontal expansion, aims to maintain current market share. Therefore, the former can generate additional exports of finished or intermediate goods from home countries, while the latter would not do so.

To test and justify the argument, regressions applied the proposed models to the three pairs of sub–samples. The resulting major findings closely relate to the major determinants of entry modes found in the previous analysis. Combining these findings leads to the following conclusions:

— First, conglomerates' foreign production of finished goods in developed countries to avoid trade friction exerts an adverse impact on parent exports to host countries. In contrast, SMEs' foreign production of intermediate goods in developing countries to exploit low labour costs has marginally positive effects on parents' exports to host countries.

— Second, the effect on affiliates' imports of intermediate goods from the home country is consistently positive and significant across different types of FDI, but it cannot be sustained for long periods because derived exports of intermediate goods will diminish over time.

— Third, delocalisation, especially for intermediate goods by SMEs, increases reverse exports to the home market. Conglomerates' foreign production of finished goods destined for third markets has adverse effects on parents' exports to those markets, but the effect is weak and not statistically significant.

These regression results indirectly support a conclusion that vertical integration and voluntary expansion have a positive impact on exports abroad while non–voluntary expansion and delocalisation have a neutral or negative impact. Overall, the empirical evidence can be interpreted as saying that differences do exist in the impact on exports of different types of foreign production.

The most notable finding of the study is that SMEs respond more sensitively to labour costs than do conglomerates, while conglomerates are more vulnerable to protective trade measures than SMEs. Restrictive trade measures characteristically trigger FDI to developed countries, while low labour costs mainly motivate FDI to developing countries. Korean firms establish production subsidiaries to manufacture finished goods, mostly consumer electronics, to circumvent restrictive trade barriers against those products, while they seek to exploit low labour costs in locating their affiliates to make intermediate goods. Restrictive trade measures exert a highly significant impact on investments of conglomerates for finished goods in developed countries, while low labour costs have a significant effect on investments of SMEs for intermediate goods in developing countries. These results are consistent with the study's hypotheses that different types of FDI have different critical determinants. Although the study does not investigate the differences in the determinants across different types of FDI, owing to difficulties associated with categorising the data by different types of FDI, the statistical findings strongly support these hypotheses.

The results of the regressions to find empirical evidence on the impact of FDI on Korean exports generally coincide with the study's hypotheses. First, substitution effects on parent exports arise in foreign production of finished goods for local sale, but the magnitude of these effects differs for different types of FDI. Second, the effect on foreign affiliates' imports of intermediate goods from Korea is consistently positive and significant across different types of FDI, but not sustainable because derived exports of intermediate goods will diminish over time. Overall, foreign production exerts opposite influences on complementary and substitute exports. Because the complementary effects of derived imports of intermediate goods prevail over the substitution effects on the exports of finished goods, the net effect is marginally positive.

The study's hypotheses on differences in the impact on exports across different types of FDI are also empirically proven. Given the problem of classification, one cannot directly verify that vertical integration and voluntary expansion have a positive impact on Korean exports abroad, or that non–voluntary expansion and delocalisation have a neutral or negative impact. The regression results do nevertheless convincingly indicate that the impact on exports is different across different types of FDI, which further suggests that the total impact of FDI on exports depends on the composition of FDI. Therefore, it is risky to prejudge FDI's substitution or complementary effects on exports without knowing the distribution of the different types of FDI.

Limitations inherent in the analysis require interpreting these findings with caution. The statistical analyses have problems associated not only with the methodology but also with the data. A cross–sectional approach has limitations in investigating a longitudinal phenomenon. Furthermore, the data come from a limited sample, and some qualitative data are based on subjective criteria. The research results need more rigorous testing, possibly with time–series data. Nevertheless, because the major statistical findings are generally consistent with each other, one can draw some policy implications from them.

The finding that dynamic positive effects prevail over the substitution effects suggests that developing countries do not need to be preoccupied, in liberalising outward FDI, with the fallacy that foreign production will bring about substitution that reduces home–country exports. Different determinants and impacts across different types of FDI, on the other hand, suggest that home countries should commit more to offensive than to defensive FDI, to protect their exports. Yet they should not necessarily adopt discriminatory incentives for offensive FDI because, when policies or regulations artificially encourage or restrict FDI, trade and FDI flows might deviate from what they would otherwise be. Instead, governments should try to eliminate or reduce restrictive host–country trade policies, probably in the negotiation process at the WTO. Such policies can cause adverse effects not only on trade but also on FDI flows. They tend to divert FDI flows to countries imposing trade barriers, which often sacrifices more viable FDI projects that otherwise could go to other regions. They thus impair not only home countries but also others that might otherwise attract FDI, eventually distorting the distribution of resources. As trade and FDI become closely intertwined, there must be international rules to ensure free flows of both. Although the WTO and OECD have made some progress in this field, coherent links between two sets of international rules must be formulated. Governments and international organisations should work towards such an objective.

The findings on differences in determinants and effects of FDI also suggest some strategic issues for corporate globalisation. They advocate that firms commit more to offensive than to defensive FDI for the sake of their better global performance. Yet the statistical analyses identified several factors motivating defensive FDI as well. Restrictive trade policies of some host countries extort investment in unviable projects. Many Korean FDI projects suffering losses were triggered mainly by these factors and reinforced by the high–leverage, growth–oriented strategies of conglomerates. As a result, after Korea's financial crisis, several Korean firms decided to withdraw from some FDI projects. These experiences provide several useful lessons in globalisation for other developing country firms:

—    First, FDI projects for corporate globalisation should be based on sound economic reasoning on a project or firm level. Defensive FDI triggered mainly by trade barriers can result in poor performance. In Korea, some defensive FDI projects relied on debt financing with such heavy guarantees by parent companies that they turned risky when parent companies became financially weakened. The current struggle of Korean industry to overcome financial weakness inevitably enhances the independent operation of their foreign affiliates and eventually leads to rationalising their foreign operations. At the same time, Korean firms will likely seek effective co–ordination of their foreign affiliates to enhance their business performance through more integrated operations. Other developing country firms can reduce learning costs when they carefully analyse these experiences.

—    Second, determining factors for FDI, especially locational ones, change rapidly. The optimisation of global production networks is not static but unstable, and the optimal location for various corporate activities can shift easily. Firms should enhance their abilities to redeploy their functions more flexibly in order to adapt to a changing business environment. They can readily redeploy final–assembly facilities without bearing substantial costs, but moving core processing or key parts manufacturing to other places involves heavy costs. Therefore, firms should be flexible in establishing foreign subsidiaries for final assembly, but cautious in making decisions to establish affiliates for core manufacturing, through careful evaluation based on long–term prospects.

— Third, developing country firms need to strengthen their firm–specific advantages in order to establish global production networks. They can do this by enhancing their own technological capabilities and improving their adaptability to new technology, which depends on the accumulation of R&D activities on core technology. Globalised firms can achieve higher rates of return by sharing newly developed core competence among many foreign affiliates. They can benefit further from using the accumulated experience of their affiliates in developing their own technology. Firms should build internal networks to secure information flows, consultancy, and technical services on technology development so that they can share technological infrastructure and knowledge.

Korean experience also suggests that other developing countries should endeavour to improve their overall business environment. In Korea, some critics insist that globalisation leads domestic firms to shift their value–added activities abroad and thus results in the hollowing out of industry. This study finds that this is not likely to occur because of the positive dynamic effects of FDI. If some adverse effects of FDI do exist, government should focus on attracting inward FDI from foreign firms rather than restricting outward FDI of domestic firms. Government does have a vital role to perform without intervening in firms' decisions. It includes:

— Building and providing the best infrastructure;

— Better education and training to develop human capital and raise firms' capacity to absorb and develop new technology;

— Establishing proper rules of the game in accordance with international standards and strictly enforcing them; and

— Improving prudent regulation and supervision to strengthen a sound economic order.

# Bibliography

ADAMS, F.G. (1992), "Empirical Estimation of the Determinants of US and Japanese FDI", Working Paper Series No. 92–2, International Centre for the Study of East Asian Development, Kitakyushu, Japan.

ANDERSSON, T. (1995), "Foreign Direct Investment and Employment in Sweden", in *Foreign Direct Investment, Trade and Employment*, OECD, Paris.

ANDERSSON, T. AND N. ARVIDSSON (1993), "Entry Modes for Direct Investment Determined by the Composition of Firm–Specific Skill*s*", The Industrial Institute for Economic and Social Research, Stockholm.

BALASSA, B. (1971), "The Structure of Protection in Developing Countries", Johns Hopkins University Press, Baltimore.

BARRELL, R. AND N. PAIN (1993), "Trade Restraints and Japanese Direct Investment Flows", *European Economic Review*, 43/1.

BARTLETT, C.A. (1984), "Organization and Control of Global Enterprise: Influences, Characteristics, and Guidelines", Graduate School of Business Administration, Harvard University, Boston, Mass.

BARTLETT, C.A. AND S. GHOSGAL (1989), "Managing Across Borders: The Transnational Solution", Harvard Business School Press, Boston, Mass.

BEHRMAN, J.N. AND W.A. FISHER (1980), "Overseas R&D Activities of Transnational Companies", OELGESCHLAGER, GUNN AND HAIN (eds.), Cambridge, Mass.

BERGSTEN, C.F., T. HORST AND T.H. MORAN (1978), "American Multinationals and American Interests", Brookings Institution, Washington, D.C.

BLOMSTRÖM, M. *et al.* (1988), "U.S. and Swedish Direct Investment and Exports", *in* R. BALDWIN (ed.), *Trade Policy Issues and Empirical Analysis*, University of Chicago Press, Chicago, Il.

BONTURI, M. AND K. FUKASAKU (1993), "Globalisation and Intra–firm Trade: An Empirical Note", *OECD Economic Studies*, No. 20.

BOYER, R. (1993), "New Directions in Management Practices and Work Organization, General Principles and National Trajectories", CEPREMAP, Paris.

BRAINARD, S.L. (1993), "An Empirical Assessment of the Proximity–Concentration Tradeoff between Multinational Sales and Trade", Working Paper No. 4580, National Bureau of Economic Research, Inc., Cambridge, Mass.

BRAINARD, S.L. (1992), "A Simple Theory of Multinational Corporations and Trade with a Tradeoff between Proximity and Concentration", MIT Sloan Working Paper No. 3492, Cambridge, Mass.

BYLINSKY, G. (1983), "The Race to the Automatic Factory", *Fortune*, Vol. 107, Issue 4, February.

CHO, D.S. (1983), "General Trading Company in Korea", Bupmunsa, Seoul, Korea.

CHO, Y. (1988), "Some Policy Lessons from the Opening of Korean Insurance Market", *World Bank Economic Review*, Vol. 2–2.

CORDEN, W.M. (1966), "The Structure of a Tariff System and the Effective Protective Rate", *Journal of Political Economy,* 64.

CULEM, C.G. (1988), "The Locational Determinants of Direct Investments Among Industrialized Countries", *European Economic Review*, 32.

CUMBY, R.E., J. HUIZINGA AND M. OBSFELD (1983), "Two–Step–Two–Stage Least Squares Estimation in Models with Rational Expectations", *Journal of Econometrics*, 21(3).

DICKEN, P. (1992), *Global Shift: The Internationalization of Economic Activity*, Paul Chapman Publishing Ltd, London.

DICKEN, P. (1991), "Europe 1992 and Strategic Change in the International Automobile Industry", *Environment and Planning,* Vol. 23.

DOZ, Y. (1987), "International Industries: Fragmentation versus Globalisation", *in* B.R. GUILE AND H. BROOKS (eds.), *Technology and Global Industries: Companies and Nations in the World Economy*, National Academy Press, Washington, D.C.

EATON, J. AND A. TAMURA (1994), "Bilateralism and Regionalism in Japanese and U.S. Trade and Direct Foreign Investment Patterns", Working Paper No. 4758, National Bureau of Economic Research, Inc., Cambridge, Mass.

EIAK (various issues), *Directory of Foreign Affiliates Established by Korean Electronics Industry*, Overseas Investment Council, Seoul, Korea.

ELECTRONICS INDUSTRY ASSOCIATION OF KOREA (EIAK) various issues, *Electronics Industry in Korea*, Seoul, Korea.

ERNST, D. (1997), "From Partial to Systemic Globalisation: International Production Networks in the Electronics Industry", BRIE Working Paper No. 98, University of California, Berkeley.

DOZ, Y. (1987), "International Industries: Fragmentation versus Globalisation", *in* B.R. GUILE AND H. BROOKS (eds.), *Technology and Global Industries: Companies and Nations in the World Economy*, National Academy Press, Washington, D.C.

FELDSTEIN, M. (1994), "The Effects of Outbound Foreign Direct Investment on the Domestic Capital Stock", Working Paper No. 4668, National Bureau of Economic Research, Boston, Mass.

GLYN, A. (1990), "Productivity and the Crisis of Fordism", *International Review of Applied Economies*, Vol. 4(1).

GREENAWAY, D. (1992), "Trade Related Investment Measures and Development Strategy", *Kyklos*, Vol. 45.

HAN, S.–T. (1992), "European Integration: The Impact on Asian Newly Industrialising Economies", working document, OECD Development Centre, Paris.

HAX, A.C. AND N.S. MAJLUF (1991), "The Strategy Concept and Process: A Pragmatic Approach", Prentice Hall, Englewood Cliffs, NJ.

HEDLUND, G. AND A. KVERNELAND (1984), "Investing in Japan – The Experience of Swedish Firms", Institute of International Business, Stockholm School of Economics, Stockholm.

HEITGER, B. AND J. STEHN (1990), "Japanese Direct Investments in the EC – Response to the Internal Market 1993", *Journal of Common Market Studies*, Basil Blackwell, Oxford, September.

HELPMAN, E. (1984), "A Simple Theory of Trade with Multinational Corporations", *Journal of Political Economy*.

HELPMAN, E AND P.R. KRUGMAN (1985), "Market Structure and Foreign Trade", MIT Press, Cambridge, Mass.

HINDLEY, B. (1994), "Contingent Protection After the Uruguay Round: Safeguards, VERs and Antidumping Action", mimeo, presented at the Chung–Hua Institution for Economic Research, Taipei.

HINDLEY, B. (1991),"The Economics of Dumping and Antidumping Action: Is there a Baby in the Bathwater?", *in* P.K.M. THARAKAN (ed.), *Policy Implications of Antidumping Measures*", Advanced Series in Management, Vol. 14.

HIRST, P. AND J. ZEITLIN (1991), "Flexible Specialisation versus Post–Fordism: Theory, Evidence and Policy Implications", *Economy and Society*, Vol. 20, No. 1, February.

HOOD, N. AND S. YOUNG (1979), *The Economics of Multinational Enterprise*, Longman, London and New York.

HORST, T. (1972), "The Industrial Composition of U.S. Exports and Subsidiary Sales to the Canadian Markets", *American Economic Review*, vol. 62, No. 1.

HORSTMANN, I.J. AND J.M. MARKUSEN (1992), "Endogenous Market Structures in International Trade", *Journal of International Economics*, 32.

HUFBAUER, G.C. AND F.M. ADLER (1968), *Overseas Manufacturing Investment and the Balance of Payments*, Tax Policy Research Study No. 1, US Treasury Dept., Washington, D.C.

HURTER, A.P. AND J.S. MARTINICH (1989), *Facility Location and the Theory of Production*, Kluwer Academic Publishers, Boston.

JAPANESE GENERAL RESEARCH INSTITUTE (1990), "Effects of Increased Overseas Direct Investment on the International Industry and Trade Structure", Tokyo.

JOHANSON, J. AND J.J. NONAKA (1983), "Japanese Export Marketing: Structure, Strategies and Counter–strategies", *International Marketing Review*, No. 1.

JOHANSON, J. AND J.–E. VAHLNE (1977), "The Internationalization Process of the Firm – A Model of Knowledge Development and Increasing Market Commitments", *Journal of International Business Studies*, Spring/Summer.

JUN, Y. (1985), *The Internationalisation Process of the Firm: The Case of the Korean Consumer Electronics Industry*, Ph.D. Dissertation, Sloan School of Management, Massachusetts Institute of Technology, Boston, Mass.

JUN, Y. (1987), "The Reverse Direct Investment: The Case of Korean Consumer Electronic Industry", *International Economic Journal*, Vol. 1, No. 3.

KANG, C.K. AND S.I. CHANG (1987), "Processing Trade and Industrial Organisation", KIET, Seoul.

KIRKPATRICK, C. AND M. YAMIN (1981), "The Determinants of Export subsidiary Formation by US Transnationals in Developing Countries: An Inter–industry Analysis", *World Development*, 9 (4).

KOBRIN, S.J. (1976), "The Environmental Determinants of Foreign Direct Manufacturing Investment: An Ex–post Empirical Analysis", *Journal of International Business Studies*, 7.

KOGUT, B. (1985), "Designing Global Strategies: Comparative and Competitive Value–added Chains", Sloan Management Review, Cambridge, Mass.

KOJIMA, K. (1982), "Macroeconomic versus International Business Approach to Direct Foreign Investment", *Hitotsubashi Journal of Economics*, Vol. 23, No.1.

KOJIMA, K. AND T. OZAWA (1985), "Toward a Theory of Industrial Restructuring and Dynamic Comparative Advantage", *Hitotsubashi Journal of Economics*, 25.

KOREA TRADE ASSOCIATION (1994), *The Impact of FDI on Trade*, Seoul.

KREININ, M.E. (1992), "Multinationalism, Regionalism, and Their Implications for Asia", Conference on Global Interdependence and Asia–Pacific Cooperation, Hong Kong.

KUMAR, N. (1987), "Intangible Assets, Internalisation and Foreign Production: Direct Investment and Licensing in Indian Manufacturing", *Weltwirtschaftliches Archiv*, 123.

LALL, S. (1990), *Building Industrial Competitiveness in Developing Countries,* OECD Development Centre Studies, Paris.

LALL, S. (in collaboration with E. CHEN, J. KATZ, B. KOSACOFF AND A. VILLELA) (1983), "The New Multinationals: The Spread of Third World Enterprises", John Wiley and Sons, Chichester and New York.

LALL, S. AND N.S. SIDDHARTHAN (1982), "The Monopolistic Advantages of Multinationals: Lessons from Foreign Investment in the US", *The Economic Journal*, Vol. 92.

LEE, B. (2000), "Foreign Direct Investment as a Vehicle for Corporate Globalisation", Doctoral Dissertation at the Institut d'études politiques, Paris.

LEE, J. (1986), "Determinants of Offshore Production in Developing Countries", *Journal of Development Economics,* Amsterdam, January/February.

LEE, C.H. AND K. LEE (1991), "A Transition Economy and Outward Direct Foreign Investment", mimeo for an APO–EWC Seminar, Seoul, Korea.

LEE, K. AND M.G. PLUMMER (1992), "Competitive Advantages, Two–Way Foreign Investment and Capital Accumulation in Korea", *Asian Economic Journal*, July.

LIPSEY, R.E. (1994), "Outward Direct Investment and the U.S. Economy", Working Paper No. 4691, National Bureau of Economic Research, Inc. Cambridge, Mass.

LIPSEY, R.E. AND M.Y. WEISS (1981), "Foreign Production and Exports in Manufacturing Industries", *Review of Economics and Statistics*, Vol LXIII, No. 4.

MADEUF, B. (1995), "Foreign Direct Investment, Trade, and Employment Delocalisation", OECD, Paris.

MARKUSEN, J.R. (1996), *A United Treatment of Horizontal Direct Investment, Vertical Direct Investment, and the Pattern of Trade in Goods and Services*, National Bureau of Economic Research, Inc., Boston, Mass.

MARKUSEN, J.R. (1991), "The Theory of the Multinational Enterprise: A Common Analytical Framework", *in* D. RAMSTETTER (ed.), *Direct Foreign Investment in Asia's Developing Economies and the Structural Change in the Asia–Pacific Region*, Westview Press, Oxford.

MARKUSEN, J.R. (1984), "Multinationals, Multi–Plant Economies and the Gain from Trade", *Journal of International Economics*, 16.

MESSERLIN, P. (1991), "The Uruguay Negotiations on Antidumping Enforcement: Some Basic Issues" *in* P.K.M. THARAKAN (ed.), *Policy Implications of Antidumping Measures*, Advanced Series in Management, Vol. 14.

MITI (JAPANESE MINISTRY OF INTERNATIONAL TRADE AND INDUSTRY) (1990), *Survey on Foreign Business Operation*, Tokyo.

MUCCHIELLI, J.L. (1992), "Déterminants de la délocalisation et firmes multinationales, analyse synthétique et application aux firmes japonaises en Europe", *Revue économique* n° 4, Paris.

MUCCHIELLI, J.L. (1985), "Les firmes multinationales: mutations et nouvelles perspectives", *Economica*, Paris.

NÖRDSTROM, K.A. (1991), "The Internationalization Process of the Firm", A Dissertation for a Doctor's Degree in Business Administration, Stockholm School of Economics, Stockholm.

OECD (1994), "Foreign Direct Investment, Trade and Employment Delocalisation", document DAFFE/IME(94)4, Paris.

OECD (1993a), *Economic Survey – Korea*, Paris.

OECD (1993b), "Globalisation of Industrial Activities, A Background Synthesis Report", document COM/DSTI/IND/TD(93)109, Paris.

OECD (1991a), "The Interrelationship of Trade and Foreign Direct Investment", OECD document TD/TC/WP(91) 51, Paris.

OECD (1991b), "Managing Manpower for Advanced Manufacturing Technology", Paris.

OECD (1989), *International Investment and Multinational Enterprises, Investment Incentives and Disincentives: Effects on International Direct Investment*, Paris, OECD.

OMAN, C. (1994), *Globalisation and Regionalisation: The Challenge for Developing Countries,* Development Centre Studies, OECD Development Centre, Paris.

OMAN, C. (1984), *New Forms of International Investment in Developing Countries,* Development Centre Studies, OECD Development Centre, Paris.

OWEN, R.F. (1982), "Inter–industry Determinants of Foreign Direct Investment: a Canadian Perspective", *in* A. RUGMAN (ed.), *New Theories of Multinational Enterprise*, Croom Helm, London.

OZAWA, T. (1990),"Europe 1992 and Japanese Multinationals: Transplanting a Subcontracting System in the Expanded Market", in B. BURGENMIER (ed.), *Multinational Firms and European Integration*, Routledge, London.

OZAWA, T. (1985), "Japan" *in* J. DUNNING (ed.), *Multinational Enterprises, Economic Structure and International Competitiveness,* John Wiley & Sons, London.

PEARCE, R., A. ISLAM AND K. SAUVANT (1992), "Determinants of Foreign Direct Investment, A Survey of the Evidence", United Nations Centre on Transnational Corporations, United Nations, New York.

PEARCE, R.D. (1989), "The Internationalisation of Sales by Leading Enterprises: Some Firm, Industry and Country Determinants", mimeo, Reading University, Reading.

PIERCY, N. (1981), "Company Internationalisation: Active and Reactive Exporting", *European Journal of Marketing*, Vol. 15, No. 3.

PORTER, M.E. (1986), *Competition in Global Industries*, Harvard Business School Press, Boston, Mass.

PUGEL, T.A. (1981), "The Determinants of Foreign Direct Investment: an Analysis of US Manufacturing Industries", *Management and Decision Economics*, 2.

REDDAWAY, W.B. *et al.* (1968), *Effects of U.K. Direct Investment Overseas*, Cambridge University Press, Cambridge.

ROOT, F.R. (1986), *Entry Strategies for International Markets*, Lexington Books, Lexington, Mass.

ROOT, F.R. AND A.A. AHMED (1979), "Empirical Determinants of Manufacturing Direct Investment in Developing Countries", *Economic Development and Cultural Change*, 27, July.

SAUNDERS, R.S. (1982), "The Determinants of Inter–industry Variation of Foreign Ownership in Canadian Manufacturing", *Canada Journal of Economics*, XV, February.

SAUVANT, K. *et al.* (1994), "Market Access Through Market Presence: Trends and Policies on Foreign Direct Investment", mimeo, OECD, Paris.

SCHNEIDER, F. AND B.S. FREY (1985), "Economic and Political Determinants of Foreign Direct Investment", *World Development*, 13, February.

SCOTT, J.J. (1994), "Safeguard", Institute for International Economics, mimeo, Washington, D.C.

SENGENBERGER, W. AND G. LOVEMAN (1987), "Smaller Units of Employment: A Synthesis Report on Industrial Reorganization in Industrialised Countries", International Institute for Labour Studies, Discussion Paper No. 3, ILO, Geneva.

STORPER, S. (1992), "Regional Development Reconsidered", *in* H. ERNSTE AND V. MEIER (eds.), *Regional Development and Contemporary Industrial Response: Extending Flexible Specialisation*, Belhaven Press, London.

SVENSSON, R. (1993), "Production in Foreign Affiliates, Effects on Home Country Exports and Modes of Entry", Industriens Utredningsinstitut, Stockholm.

SWEDENBORG, B. (1985), "Sweden", *in* J. DUNNING (ed.), *Multinational Enterprises, Economic Structure and International Competitiveness*, John Wiley & Sons, London.

SWEDENBORG, B. (1979), "The Multinational Operations of Swedish Firms. An Analysis of Determinants and Effects", The Industrial Institute for Economic and Social Research, Stockholm.

UNCTAD, *World Investment Report*, various issues, Geneva.

UNCTAD (1995), *World Investment Report 1995; Transnational Corporations and Competitiveness*, Geneva.

UNCTAD (1992), *World Investment Report 1992: Transnational Corporations as Engines of Growth*, Geneva.

UNITED NATIONS (1993), *Transnational Corporations from Developing Countries: Impact on their Home Countries*, New York.

UNITED NATIONS (1992), *The Determinants of Foreign Direct Investment*, New York.

WELLS, L.T. (1983), "Third World Multinationals", MIT Press, Cambridge, Mass.

WHEELER, D. AND A. MODY (1992) "International Investment Location Decisions: The Case of U.S. Firms", *Journal of International Economics*.

WTO (1994), *1994 Report on Unfair Trade Policies by Major Trading Partners*, a report of the WTO Subcommittee on Unfair Trade Policies and Measures, WTO, Geneva.

YANNOPOULOS, G.N. (1990), "Foreign Direct Investment and European Integration: The Evidence from the Formative Years of the European Community", *Journal of Common Market Studies*, March.

YEATS, A. (1979), *Trade Barriers Facing Developing Countries*, Macmillan Press Ltd., London.

OECD PUBLICATIONS, 2, rue André-Pascal, 75775 PARIS CEDEX 16
PRINTED IN FRANCE
(41 2002 04 1P) ISBN 92-64-19809-1 – No. 52557 2002